MUSCLE
CARS

A Legacy of American Performance

CREDITS

We would like to thank the following vehicle owners and photographers for supplying the images in this book.

1962 Chevrolet: O: Tony Garcia; P: Vince Manocchi. **1962 Ford:** O: Terry Davis; P: Doug Mitchel. **1962 Plymouth:** O: Rich rd Levin; P: Jeff Cohn. **1963 Chevrolet:** O: Steve Schultz; P: Nick Komic. **1963 Dodge:** O: Denny Guest; P: Doug Mitchel **1963 Ford:** O: Kenneth Kowalk; P: Al Rogers. **1963 Pontiac:** O: Randy & Jean Williams; P: Doug Mitchel. **1963 Studebak r:** O: Nelson Bove; P: Gary Kessler. **1964 Chevrolet:** O: Duffy's Collectible Cars; P: Robert Nicholson. **1964 Ford Fairlan** : Donald Allen; P: Al Rogers. **1964 Ford Galaxie:** O: David Temple; P: David Temple. **1964 Plymouth:** O: Richard Horner; : Paul Zazarine. **1964 Pontiac:** O: Brian Thomason; P: Mike Spenner. **1964 Studebaker:** O: Nelson Bove; P: Gary Kes- ler. **1965 Dodge Coronet:** O: Robert Mosher; P: Vince Manocchi. **1965 Dodge Dart:** O: Robert Ferguson; P: Vince Man- cchi. **1965 Ford Custom 500:** O: Mike Patak; P: David Temple. **1965 Ford Mustang:** O: Craig Chesley; P: David Temple. **1965 Oldsmobile:** O: Donald Senek; P: Doug Mitchel. **1966 Chevrolet:** O: Chris Piscitello; P: David Temple. **1966 Dodge:** : Frank Zilka; P: Doug Mitchel. **1966 Ford:** O: Douglas Lombardo; P: Doug Mitchel. **1966 Mercury:** O: James Ladewig; : Al Rogers. **1966 Plymouth:** O: Nicolas Balli Jean; P: Al Rogers. **1966 Pontiac:** O: Arnold Boris; P: Doug Mitchel. **1967 uick:** O: Motorcar Portfolio; P: Brandon Hemphill. **1967 Chevrolet Camaro:** O: Bill Clemens; P: Al Rogers. **1967 Chevro- t Impala:** O: Ronald Mroz; P: Roger Mattingly. **1967 Dodge:** O: Mike Spencer; P: Doug Mitchel. **1967 Plymouth:** O: Tom hinn; P: David Temple. **1967 Pontiac:** O: RK Motors Charlotte; P: Al Rogers. **1968 Chevrolet:** O: Duffy's Collectible Cars Robert Nicholson. **1968 Dodge:** O: David Freeman; P: Doug Mitchel. **1968 Ford:** O: Terry Nelson; P: Doug Mitchel. **196 dsmobile:** O: Anthony Curro; P: Thomas Glatch. **1968 Plymouth:** O: Mike Ventrone; P: Ryan Conaty. **1968 Shelby:** O: Ke eth Nagel; P: Al Rogers. **1969 AMC S/C Rambler:** O: Frank Indriso; P: Howard Korn. **1969 AMC Javelin:** O: John Robert n; P: Doug Mitchel. **1969 Chevrolet Camaro:** O: RK Motors Charlotte; P: Al Rogers. **1969 Chevrolet Chevelle:** O: Steve chultz; P: Nick Komic. **1969 Chevrolet Impala:** O: Arnold Boris; P: Doug Mitchel. **1969 Dodge Charger:** O: RK Motors harlotte; P: Al Rogers. **1969 Dodge Super Bee:** O: Dan Varner; P: Al Rogers. **1969 Ford:** O: Rick Campbell; P: Al Rogers. **1969 Mercury:** O: Michael Mennela; P: Doug Mitchel. **1969 Oldsmobile:** O: Northwest Auto Sales; P: Brandon Hemphill. **1969 Plymouth Barracuda:** O: Mutual Fun Investments; P: David Temple. **1969 Plymouth Roadrunner:** O: Roy Cordrey; P: ug Mitchel. **1969 Pontiac GTO:** O: Bill Schultz; P: Al Rogers. **1969 Pontiac Firebird:** O: RK Motors Charlotte; P: Al Rog- s. **1970 AMC:** O: Patrick Wnek; P: Thomas Glatch. **1970 Chevrolet:** O: Tom Chinn; P: David Temple. **1970 Dodge Chal- ger:** O: Gilmore Museum; P: Nick Komic. **1970 Dodge Super Bee:** O: FCA Historical Services; P: Al Rogers. **1970 Ford ustang:** O: Mike Bolf; P: Nick Komic. **1970 Ford Ranchero:** O: David Tess; P: Doug Mitchel. **1970 Ford Torino:** O: John Carthy; P: Doug Mitchel. **1970 Mercury:** O: Rich Ladd; P: Vince Manocchi. **1970 Oldsmobile:** O: Tom Chinn; P: David mple. **1970 Plymouth 'Cuda:** O: Tom Chinn; P: David Temple. **1970 Plymouth Superbird:** O: John Gastman; P: Doug tchel. **1971 AMC:** O: Peter Cambrola; P: Leigh Dorrington. **1971 Buick:** O: Paul Pierce; P: Dan Lyons. **1971 Chevrolet:** Dale Schieman; P: Doug Mitchel. **1971 Plymouth:** O: Otto Groth; P: Doug Mitchel. **1971 Pontiac:** O: Tom Chinn; P: Davi mple. **1972 Ford:** O: Nick Dominick; P: Howard Korn. **1972 Oldsmobile:** O: Tom Chinn; P: David Temple. **1973 Chevrolet** Leroy & Judy Williams; P: W.C. Waymack. **1973 Dodge:** O: Judy Williamson; P: Doug Mitchel. **1973 Ford:** O: Shane & mmy Braynt; P: Ken Beebe. **1973 Plymouth:** O: Doug Vura; P: Vince Manocchi. **1974 Chevrolet:** O: John Oehler; P: Doug tchel. **1976 Oldsmobile:** O: Larry Simoulis; P: Doug Mitchel. **1978 Ford:** O: Russell Lehart; P: David Temple. **1979 Pon- c:** O: RK Motors Charlotte; P: Al Rogers.

CONTENTS

INTRODUCTION

To those who loved them—those who could recognize a super car with just a glance at a fender emblem—it was as if the streets in the Sixties and early Seventies were alive with muscle. Cars with roaring exhausts seemed to squeal away from every stoplight in America.

The muscle car era had its roots in the postwar Detroit horsepower race and peaked in 1970, when every major American automaker offered a 340-450-horsepower super car. In reality, the number of bonafide muscle cars was quite low when counted against the millions of automobiles that Detroit was churning out. Unfortunately, high insurance rates, rising gas prices, and increasing government regulation quickly made these factory hot rods obsolete.

If the lore of muscle cars is out of proportion to their actual numbers, that merely underscores their impact. Indeed, these machines created an entire culture, with its own language and customs, heroes and pretenders. It is to those who loved these cars—and to those just discovering their magic—that *Muscle Cars* is dedicated.

By the strictest definition, a muscle car was a rear-wheel-drive midsize two-door coupe or sedan with a powerful V-8 engine. Here, we recognize that, however, any worthwhile treatment of the subject must go beyond such a confining interpretation. What really mattered was the car's use of horsepower to break away from ordinary daily transportation.

So here you'll find not only GTOs and GTXs, but Camaros and Javelins, Mustangs and 'Cudas, Galaxies and Impalas, and even a couple Studebakers. We also take a quick trip through the post-1971 landscape to better illustrate how quickly it all fell apart before the first glimmers of a new era of muscle started to appear in the Eighties.

The Editors of Consumer Guide Automotive
Morton Grove, Illinois
April 2017

1962 CHEVROLET IMPALA SS

Though most drag racers favored Chevy's cheaper, lighter Bel Air "bubbletop," the 1962 Impala two-door hardtop cut a sharp figure as well, especially in SS guise. The formal roofline of the hardtop mimicked the look of a top-up convertible. The Impala's flashier trim was highlighted by a brushed-aluminum rear cove with six taillights instead of the Bel Air's four.

After limited exposure in 1961, the Turbo-Fire 409 V-8 was now a regular-production option. Compared to the seldom-seen '61 edition, it had a stronger block and tougher cast-alloy heads, along with revised pistons. Adding a base single-quad 380-horsepower 409 to any full-size Chevy added $428 to the price. Dual Carter AFB four-barrel carbs raised horsepower to 409 for only $60 more. The four-speed transmission was another $188 over the base three speed.

Super Sport Impalas could be recognized from the outside by their "SS" emblems and anodized aluminum bodyside moldings. Crossed flags above the 409 emblems on the front fenders marked these Impalas as machines to be respected. Normally SS Impalas wore full-face wheelcovers, but this one sports Bel Air-style "dog-dish" hubcaps for a bit tougher vibe.

On the Impala, front bucket seats were a $102 option and were often ordered with the Super Sport package. The SS package itself was a $54 option for Sport Coupes or convertibles and again included a center console on the floor and a passenger grip bar. A tachometer was another factory option, and it came mounted on the steering column.

1962 FORD GALAXIE

Ford began 1962 without an engine over 400 cubic inches, a serious deficiency against the formidable 409 Chevrolets, 413 Mopars, and 421 Pontiacs. The remedy came partway through the selling season with an enlargement of Ford's 390-cid V-8 to 406 cubic inches.

Called the Thunderbird 406 High-Performance V-8, but available only in the Galaxie, the new engine cost $380 and came with a heavy-duty suspension, fade-resistant drum brakes, high-capacity radiator, and 15-inch wheels instead of the regular 14s.

Breathing through a single Holley four-barrel, the 406 had 385 horsepower and 440 lb-ft of torque. As the Super High-Performance Tri-Power, it put three Holley two-barrels under a lovely oval air cleaner and was rated at 405 horsepower. Both had cast-iron headers and low-restriction dual exhausts.

A 385-horse 406 would scoot to 60 mph in 7.1 seconds; the tri-power was about a half-second quicker. Quarter-mile times in the mid-15s were the rule.

In sanctioned drag racing, the 406 Fords were still too heavy to outrun the top guns from Dodge, Plymouth, Chevy, and Pontiac. Ford shaved 164 pounds off special competition versions by offering aluminum bumpers and fiberglass body panels, but it just wasn't enough.

On the street though, a rival who didn't notice the gold "406" emblem on the front fender could easily get caught napping by one of these fortified Galaxies. The 406 was also made available in the big Mercurys by late '62.

1962 PLYMOUTH SAVOY

Like corporate-cousin Dodge, Plymouth struggled in 1962 with controversial styling. Seven inches shorter and up to 400 pounds lighter than a '61 model, the new cars were available with several performance V-8s. These started with a 361-cubic-inch job with dual four-barrel carbs and 310 horsepower. Above this were 383 V-8s with a single four barrel rated at 330 horses and another with dual quads and 335 ponies. Then came 413s with a single four barrel and 365 horsepower or 380 with dual quads.

Those who wanted to go seriously fast could look to the available top-shelf 410-horsepower 413 V-8. Plymouth dubbed its version of this wedge-head engine the Super Stock 413, no doubt in honor of the Super Stock classes these Mopars soon ruled at the nation's drag strips.

Relatively few of these so-called "Max Wedge" 413s were built. Though the Savoy featured here packs the 335-horse 383, many of the Max Wedges that were ordered went into bare-bones two-door sedans like this one. No stripes. No badges. Just thunder waiting to happen. It's a classic example of the unassuming look preferred by serious street racers.

At around 3200 pounds the Savoy weighed even less than its Dodge cousin, and could be lightened further still by being ordered without heater, radio, and sound deadening. In a Savoy, both the grocery-getter and go-getter shared the simplest of gauges and controls. A quick stab at the gas though would quickly make clear how much muscle was under the hood.

1963 CHEVROLET IMPALA Z-11

Chevrolet's bubble-roof 1962 Bel Air hardtop was gone for '63, leaving only the squared-off Impala as a pillarless two door. Deceptively ordinary, this silver '63 Impala actually is one of the special-production "Z-11" drag cars.

With a limited run of just 57 examples, the Z-11 was Chevrolet's entry into the lightweight factory race-car game. All carried a stroked 427-cubic-inch version of the 409 with dual-four-barrel carburetors and a very conservative factory rating of 430 horsepower at 6000 rpm and 425 pound-feet of torque at 4200. Z-11s also used a special air cleaner/plenum assembly that ducted fresh air in from the cowl vent. The 427-cube engine matched the new NASCAR and NHRA displacement limits.

Extensive weight-cutting measures included the deletion of the radio, heater, and insulation, plus aluminum front fenders and inner fenders, hood, radiator support panel and fan shroud, and bumpers and their brackets. All this helped bring down weight by about 140 pounds.

Of course, Chevy's plans changed in early 1963 when GM's upper management told all of the company's divisions to cease racing activities. This meant Z-11 production stopped before enough copies were made to make the cars legal for NHRA Super Stock class competition. The NASCAR effort with a different "Mystery" 427 V-8 was nipped in the bud too.

The "civilian" 1963 Chevrolet engine roster topped out at a 425-horsepower 409. Bucket-seat Impala SS (Super Sport) models were popular on the street.

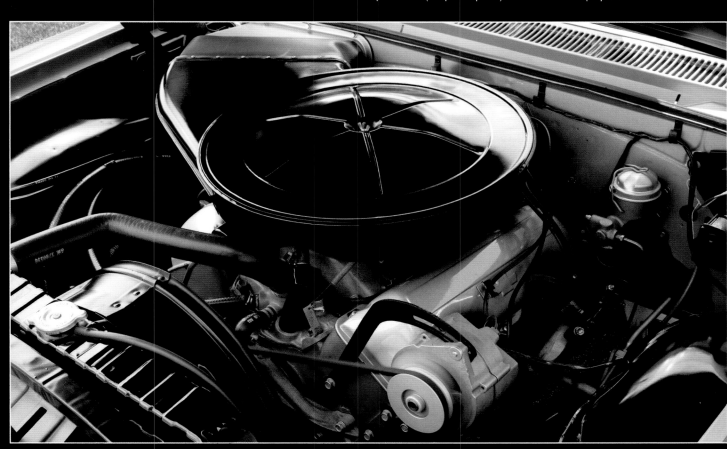

1963 DODGE 330

Sagging sales of the 1962 models taught Dodge its lesson. Styling for '63 was cleaned up and toned down, and the wheelbase of its standard-size cars grew by three inches to 119. The series were called 330 (shown) , 440, and Polara. For the go-fast bunch, there was welcome news under the hood too.

The new 426-cubic-inch "Wedge" was basically a bored 413, again called Ramcharger at Dodge and Super Stock at Plymouth. Dual Carter four-barrels and upswept ram's-head exhaust headers were retained. But the 426 benefitted from a host of internal beef-ups to make 415 horsepower on 11.0:1 compression or 425 ponies on 13.5:1. Stage III 425-horse versions followed during the year with further tweaks including larger-bore carbs, recast cylinder heads, and 12.5:1 compression.

The preferred transmission choice was a heavy-duty TorqueFlite automatic, which again used push-button gear selection. The alternative was a floor-shift three-speed manual; Chrysler didn't have a four-speed yet.

This was serious ordinance, and ill-suited for everyday use. Indeed, even the brochures warned that the 426 warmed up slowly and was "not a street machine" but was "designed to be run in supervised, sanctioned drag-strip competition....Yet, it is stock in every sense of the word."

Factory-built light-weight racers wore an aluminum front end and made do without the radio and heater. Quarter-mile times under 13 seconds were very possible at the track.

1963 FORD FAIRLANE 500

The best-remembered of Ford's "1963 1/2" midyear product additions are almost certainly the Sports Hardtop semi-fastback Galaxie two-door hardtops. The legendary 427-cubic-inch V-8 was another midyear intro.

Ford's midsize Fairlane received a performance upgrade of its own in mid-1963 with the introduction of the thrilling "High-Performance" 289-cubic-inch V-8 with 271 horsepower and 312 pound-feet of torque. Performance goodies on the new mill included a four-barrel carburetor, solid-lifter cam, and header-style exhaust manifolds. Modified heads ran 11.0:1 compression. The new 289 could only be ordered with a 4-speed manual transmission.

The "Hi-Po" 289 was a natural fit for the Fairlane, given that it was the third-basic version of the 221-cube "small-block" V-8 that Ford conjured up for the Fairlane's 1962 debut. The 271-horse 289 could move a Fairlane from 0-60 mph in less than 9 seconds.

Fairlane offered only two- and four-door sedan bodies when it was introduced for 1962. Along with freshened styling that closely followed the frontal appearance of the year's full-size Ford, Fairlane added a two-door hardtop and a four-door wagon for its sophomore season.

The featured car is the top Sport Coupe hardtop that added bucket seats, console, spinner wheel covers, and Sport Coupe script on the decklid. It was the only '63 Fairlane to wear the three Buick-style "ventiports" on each front fender. New, this car priced out at $3415.30.

1963 PONTIAC TEMPEST STATION WAGON

1963 PONTIAC TEMPEST STATION WAGON

By 1963, Super Stock drag racing was a phenomenon, capturing the attention of manufacturers, competitors, and spectators, all of them wanting to definitively say which company made the fastest cars around. Pontiac started the Sixties strongly with its Super Duty parts program and factory-built SD Catalina and Grand Prix racers. The lighter 426-cubic-inch Dodges and Plymouths proved serious foes at the strip though.

The idea of dropping Pontiac's brutal 421-cubic-inch Super Duty race V-8 into the compact Tempest surfaced in 1962. Racer Mickey Thompson, legendary Detroit-area dealer Royal Pontiac, and even Pontiac Engineering all cooked up their own takes on the idea.

Pontiac eventually built two Tempest coupe prototypes, six LeMans coupes, and—amazingly—six Tempest station wagons. The goal with the wagons was to get extra weight over the rear wheels to help with traction. All had full aluminum front ends and doors lightened by leaving out most of the inner bracing.

Power came from a unique version of the 421 SD engine with a lower-profile dual-quad intake that was rated at 405 horsepower. Folks in the know said real output was more like 500 ponies. The engine mated to a specially built "Power-shift" 4-speed transaxle mounted in the rear of the car.

Unfortunately, all the effort was nipped in the bud. On January 24, 1963, General Motors announced that the company was pulling out of all factory-backed racing activities.

1963 STUDEBAKER GRAN TURISMO HAWK

1963 STUDEBAKER GRAN TURISMO HAWK

Studebaker performance can be traced back to the 1956 Golden Hawk. It was an updated version of the company's famous 1953 "Loewy" Starliner hardtop fitted with a 275-horsepower Packard V-8 that displaced 352 cubic inches. Unfortunately, Packard production in Detroit ended during 1956, which meant the big V-8 was no longer available. For the 1957 Golden Hawk, Studebaker fitted a McCulloch Jet-Stream centrifugal supercharger to the its 289-cubic-inch V-8. It was also rated at 275 ponies. Golden Hawk production ended with the 1958 models, taking the supercharged 289 with it. The Hawk series continued as a pillared coupe through 1961, but with no more than 225 horsepower.

Designer Brooks Stevens gave the Hawk a classy update for 1962. He returned it to a true hardtop with a sharp new "Thunderbird-style" roofline and also relieved the car of its fender fins. The resulting car was called the Gran Turismo Hawk and remained in production through 1964.

Studebaker raised the high-performance ante for the 1963 models with the arrival of R-Series engines. These were developed for the then-new Avanti sports coupe, and the company also offered them in the Lark and Gran Turismo Hawk.

The featured 1963 GT Hawk is fitted with the optional R2 version of the 289 V-8. It was fitted with a Paxton SN-60 supercharger that was smaller and lighter than the blower used in the Fifties. The R2's carburetor was fitted with a chrome bonnet to direct pressurized air from the supercharger into the internally sealed carb. Output was 289 horsepower—exactly one horsepower per cubic inch.

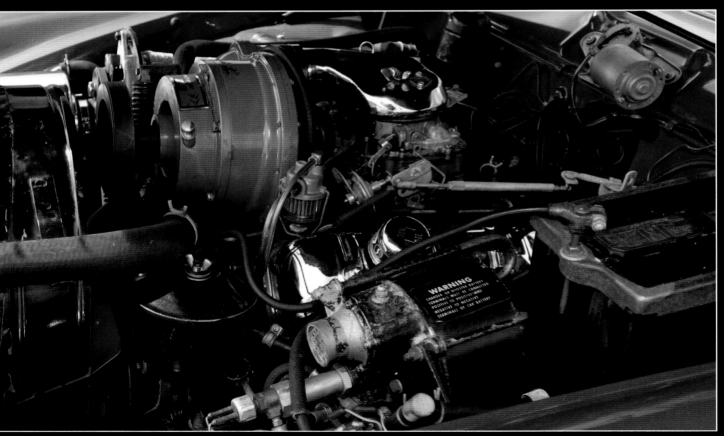

1964 CHEVROLET NOVA SS

Following a successful introductory season as a 1962 model, 1963 was a year of enhancement for the Chevy II. The biggest news was the introduction of an attractive Nova Super Sport option for the Sport Coupe two-door hardtop and convertible. It followed the pattern set by the 1962 Impala SS, and included a full-vinyl interior with front bucket seats, full instrumentation, 14-inch wheels with full "SS" wheel covers, and distinctive exterior trim. The top engine choice was a 120-horsepower "Hi-Thrift" six cylinder, which just couldn't compete with the mid-year Ford Falcon Sprint and its 260 V-8.

The spring of 1963 was marked with speculation that the Chevy II would be discontinued to make way for the upcoming mid-size 1964 Chevelle. That was the original plan, but high sales in '63 earned the Chevy II a reprieve for 1964. There was good news and bad.

The good news was that Chevy's 195-horsepower 283-cubic-inch V-8 and a 4-speed manual transmission joined the options list. It would have been a fine addition to the Nova SS, but the problem was that the SS had been dropped.

Chevy actually dropped all Chevy II hardtops and convertibles, leaving the sportiest Nova a two-door sedan. Then Chevy reconsidered and reinstated the Nova Sport Coupe hardtop and Super Sport hardtops in early 1964.

For the remainder of the 1964 model year, demand for Nova SS hardtops was brisk. Performance was further improved thanks to the four-barrel 220-horsepower 283 V-8 that was also announced mid-year.

1964 FORD FAIRLANE THUNDERBOLT

1964 FORD FAIRLANE THUNDERBOLT

Even with their strong 427-cubic-inch V-8s and lightened front ends, big body-on-frame Ford Galaxies were no match for the lighter-still unibody Dodges and Plymouths. The obvious solution was to stuff the mighty 427 into the midsize Fairlane. Nothing good comes easy though. With help from Dearborn Steel Tubing, a contract car builder, Ford concocted the race-ready and street-legal, if not exactly streetable, Thunderbolt.

Extensive front-end modifications were necessary to custom-fit the big-block, and eight equal-length exhaust headers had to be snaked through the suspension components. The competition 427's high-rise intake manifold elevated the aircleaner above the fenderline, which made a teardrop-shaped hood bubble mandatory. The engine gulped air through screens fit into the inner headlight bezels. Transmissions were a Hurst-shifted four-speed or a beefy automatic. Massive traction bars, asymmetrical rear springs, and a trunk-mounted 95-pound bus battery helped get down what was realistically 500 horsepower.

Weight cutting was merciless: plexiglass windows, and fiberglass front body panels, bumpers, and doors. Sunvisors, mirror, sound-deadener, armrests—even the jack and lug wrench—were shed. The back seat remained, but the fronts were lightweight buckets from the Econoline truck.

At 3225 pounds, the T-Bolt did weigh more than a stock Fairlane. But it was only 20 pounds over its NHRA class minimum. At last, Ford had a winner. ETs in the 11s earned the Top Stock crown and the NHRA Manufacturer's Cup in '64.

1964 FORD GALAXIE 500/XL

The 1964 Ford was the last model that had its origins in the 118-inch wheelbase 1957 Fairlane. While body styling changed dramatically during this run, inner body panels and floor pans changed very little. Wheelbase increased to 119 inches in 1960, and that's the span the '64s used.

The fresh face Ford showed for 1964 was inspired by a number of the company's aerodynamically styled show cars of the period. Highlights included "pontoon" bodyside sculpting, a longer rear deck, rounded nose, and a horizontal-bar grille with three distinct vertical peaks. Taillights remained round, but were now sunken into a sharply edged rear cove.

The previous Galaxie and 300 names were retired at the bottom end of the lineup, and were replaced with Custom and Custom 500. Galaxie 500 and the bucket-seat XL subseries continued at the top.

Performance on the street was good for the time. With a 390-cubic-inch V-8, 0-60 mph times of 9.3 seconds were possible. The top 427 V-8s could improve this sprint to 7.4 seconds which was pretty remarkable for a two-ton car.

This wasn't enough for dragstrip dominance though, so despite a small run of factory lightweight Galaxies, the Fairlane-based Thunderbolts were Ford's primary weapon against the speedy Dodges and Plymouths on the strip.

The big Fords did better in Grand National stock-car racing though, even though Mopar's Hemi captured most of the spotlight there too. Still, at the end of the season, Ford topped the winner's chart with 30 victories.

1964 PLYMOUTH BELVEDERE

For 1964, Plymouth sported a fresh clean look, thanks to Elwood Engel and his staff's second facelift on the basic body used for Plymouth's ill-conceived downsized 1962 models. Most of the work centered on new peaked front fenders and a grille that followed the same theme. Two-door hardtops also wore a new roof profile with narrower rear pillars and a wrap-around rear window. As a whole, the resulting '64 Plymouth was quite handsome.

The lineup started with the plain-Jane Savoy, and moved up to the Belvedere, Fury, and top-line Sport Fury. Body styles included two- and four-door sedans and hardtops, a four-door station wagon, and a convertible.

Underhood, buyers could choose from engines in five different displacements. Smallest was a 225-cubic-inch version of Chrysler's "Slant Six," rated at 145 horsepower. The rest were V-8s of 318, 361, 383, and 426 cubic inches. The 426 had wedge-shaped combustion chambers and came tuned for 365, 415, or 425 horsepower. The top two versions had dual four-barrel carbs on a cross-ram intake manifold. Buyers could chose from a four-speed manual transmission with Hurst linkage or the proven TorqueFlite three-speed automatic.

Like corporate-cousin Dodge, Plymouth's racetrack performance increased notably with the introduction of the 426 Hemi V-8 in early 1964. Success arrived quickly with the Hemi powering Richard Petty's Plymouth to victory in the Daytona 500. Streetable versions of the Hemi wouldn't arrive until 1966 though, so until then the hot set-up on the street remained the 426 Wedge.

1964 PONTIAC TEMPEST GTO

The Big Bang in modern muscle's evolution is the 1964 Pontiac GTO. This is where it began: a midsize automobile with a big, high-power V-8 marketed as an integrated high-performance package—the very definition of a muscle car.

To create the GTO, Pontiac sidestepped GM's prohibition on intermediate-sized cars having engines over 330-cubic inches. In a ploy that didn't require corporate approval, Pontiac included its 389 V-8 as part of a $296 option package for the new Tempest. The name Gran Turismo Omologato was boldly appropriated from the Ferrari GTO. Roughly translated, it means a production grand touring machine sanctioned for competition.

To create an engine worthy of this machine, Pontiac fortified the 389 with a high-lift cam and the 421 V-8's high-output heads. The GTO had 325 horsepower with the standard Carter four-barrel carb. The extra-cost Tri-Power setup delivered a trio of Rochester two-barrels and 348 ponies. The standard three-speed manual and optional four-speed used Hurst linkages. There was also an available two-speed automatic.

A thick sway bar, heavy-duty shocks, stiffened springs, and high-speed 14-inch tires were included. The sporting attitude continued inside, where all GTOs had front bucket seats and an engine-turned aluminum instrument surround.

Pontiac hoped to move 5000 '64 GTOs: it actually sold 32,450. The Goat, as it was affectionately dubbed, generated a cult following and sent rivals scrambling to come up with similar machines.

1964 STUDEBAKER COMMANDER

For 1964, Studebaker enlisted Brooks Stevens to give the Lark compact a handsome facelift that made the aging bodies look like they were brand new. Overall length was up by six inches; the grille became more horizontal, with an eggcrate center and integral headlights; and a pointy new rear end carried high-set taillight assemblies. The Lark name was being downplayed to the point that it actually didn't appear on the car.

The four-speed Commander two-door sedan featured here is the only non-Avanti 1964 Studebaker to be equipped from the factory with the supercharged 304.5-cubic-inch R3 engine. The V-8 was rated at 335 horsepower, but period magazine reviewers suspected that the actual output was substantially higher.

The R3 engine was the most powerful Studebaker V-8 ever marketed. They started with select blocks from the South Bend foundry that were carefully bored .093 of an inch over. Large-valve heads were fitted. A pressure box fully enclosed a single carburetor on an aluminum intake manifold. There was also a transistorized ignition system and cast-iron headers. All production R3 engines were built under the supervision of the famous Granatelli brothers at Paxton Products in Santa Monica, California.

On December 31, 1963, Studebaker ended automobile manufacturing operations in South Bend, Indiana. New Year's Eve also marked the end of Studebaker's run of factory-built performance cars. For all practical purposes, passenger-car production shifted to the company's more-modern facility in Hamilton, Ontario, Canada on January 1, 1964. Production would continue there for a little more than two years, until Studebaker itself folded.

1965 DODGE CORONET A990

In late 1964, Chrysler announced its program for 1965 to build a strictly limited run of intermediate-sized specials for use in drag racing—or, in Chrysler's words "supervised acceleration trials and other competitive events." Bearing the order code A990, the cars chosen for the job were the Plymouth Belvedere I and base Dodge Coronet two-door sedans equipped with the 426-cubic-inch Hemi V-8 under their scooped hoods.

The Hemi, which was still a year away from general availability as an option in B-body cars, contained a number of parts designed to reduce weight. These included a cast-magnesium ram-tuned intake manifold, plus cylinder heads and oil-pump housing and cover in cast aluminum. Two Holley four-barrel carbs were topped with a single oval-shaped air cleaner. Horsepower was modestly rated at 425, and Dodge called this engine the "Hemi-Charger."

Since the National Hot Rod Association (NHRA) had banned aluminum body parts and plexiglass windows, Chrysler used 40-percent thinner lightweight steel instead. On the Coronets, the inner pair of headlamps were deleted. All A990s had lightweight interior trim and seats, and the order sheet required that the heater and rear seat belts be deleted.

These cars were sold "as is" with no warranty, and prospective customers had to sign a document acknowledging that. Customers were further warned that these cars "are not intended for highway or general passenger car use." None of this was a surprise to the intended owners, of course.

1965 DODGE DART GT CHARGER 273

GT trim sharpened Dodge's milquetoast Dart for 1965. In addition, Darts wore a facelift with a brash eggcrate grille, and there was an interesting partial vinyl roof option for the hardtop. These compacts rode a 111-inch wheelbase. The GT was available for 1964 with a two-barrel 273-cubic-inch V-8 good for a modest 180 horsepower. For '65, the GT had a 235-horse version of the 273 paired with a standard three-speed gearbox, optional four-speed, or TorqueFlite three-speed automatic.

Dart GT's free-revving, short-stroke, hydraulic-lifter 273 used a Carter AFB four-barrel and 10.5:1 compression. It only cost $99.40 extra. *Car and Driver* managed 8.2 seconds 0-60 mph and a 16.9-second quarter at 87 mph with their GT hardtop test car. A four-speed may have been first choice of stoplight strokers, but the magazine review stated that the TorqueFlite was "one automatic transmission that can actually be shifted," giving it "overwhelming superiority over manual units in super stock drag racing."

On the surface, a Dart GT was a dressed-for-success Dart 270 with bucket seats, extra chrome, and a stylized badge. Other GT touches included rocker-panel vents. Real five-spoke Cragar mags and the high-output 273 V-8 were included on the rare limited-production Charger 273 variant, which was made primarily for the Southern California market.

The Dart GT hardtop had a base price of $2372, while the ragtop started at $2591. Total Dart GT production for '65 was 45,118.

1965 FORD CUSTOM 500

1965 FORD CUSTOM 500

The 1965 models were the most changed Fords since 1949, if not the most changed in the company's history. They were truly new from the ground up, with a stronger frame and coil-spring suspension front and rear. The sturdy front suspension became the go-to design for NASCAR racers of all brands through the 1970s. The rugged new nine-inch rear axle was similarly prized by racers and hot rodders.

The styling was cleaner with more stately lines, and a horizontal-bar grille flanked by stacked quad headlamps led the way. At the rear most models used new roughly hexagonal taillamp shape, but low-line models had the traditional round lenses inside the new-shape bezel.

The flashy street cars were the Galaxie 500/XL hardtops and convertibles, with the hardtop being the bodystyle of choice for Ford's hugely successful 1965 NASCAR stock-car racing efforts.

Serious street racers might have been more drawn to the lower-cost two-door sedans. Ford still offered the mighty R-Code 425-horsepower 427 engine in its full-size machines. Production was very limited though, and the mid-level Custom 500 shown here may be one of only three that were built. This car also wears the glass headlight covers that were standard on 427-powered full-size '65 Fords.

The performance market was shifting away from full-size models though, and quickly. The mid-season debut of the posh LTD was a clear forecast of where full-size Fords were heading. Buyers choose the new way, and LTD's success made Ford's emphasis on full-size luxury inevitable.

1965 FORD MUSTANG

The formula for the Ford Mustang was simple: a reasonably priced, sporty, personal car based on high-volume Falcon components. Riding a compact 108-inch wheelbase, Mustang pioneered the pony-car concept with its long-hood/short-deck silhouette, bucket-seat interior, and long options list.

Prices started at $2372 for a hardtop coupe and $2614 for the convertible, putting Mustang within the reach of a huge swath of new-car buyers. Those with deep pockets could personalize their Mustang through the wide array of luxury and performance options.

Here, we're most interested in the go-fast goodies. The Hi-Performance 271-horsepower 289 cubic-inch V-8 was the ultimate factory powerplant. It featured high-compression cylinder heads, a high-lift camshaft, free-breathing air intake system, free-flow exhaust, solid valve lifters, and chrome-plated valve stems. The engine could be further fortified with several extra-cost "kits" that added goodies like a racier cam or larger valves with stouter springs.

Though Mustang was certainly attractive, it was not exotic or earth-shaking in appearance. Properly optioned, however, the Mustang could certainly move. *Road & Track* tested a 271-horsepower model and found brisk acceleration of 8.5 seconds from 0-60 mph. The quarter-mile dash took 15.6 seconds at 85 mph, and top speed was 120.

Total Mustang production for 1965 was 680,989 units. This broke down into 77,079 2+2 fastbacks, 101,945 convertibles, and 501,965 hardtops.

1965 OLDSMOBILE 4-4-2

Oldsmobile took the hint. Shuffling onto the burgeoning performance scene in mid 1964 with a "police package" that could be ordered on a four-door sedan was no recipe for muscle-car success. Indeed, fewer than 3000 of the original 4-4-2s were sold.

The strategy was refined for 1965. Olds made the 4-4-2 an option on the F-85 pillared two-door coupe, along with the nicer Cutlass coupe, two-door hardtop, and convertible. Styling was updated, and the 4-4-2 was distinguished with chrome bodyside tires.

Marketing was hipper, too. Instead of a couple cops in a bland '64 sedan, 4-4-2 advertising for '65 was filled with references to cubic inches and horsepower. Buzzwords like "kicks" and "cool" flew freely. One spot showed nothing but blurred asphalt and the declaration, "Olds 4-4-2 was here!"

GM itself got the message too, and relaxed the displacement ceiling on intermediates to 400 cubic inches. Olds destroked and debored its new big-car 425-cubic-inch V-8 to create a hot 400 that was exclusive to the 4-4-2. It was good for 345 horsepower and 440 lb-ft of torque. Now the name meant 400 cubes, four-barrel carb, and dual exhausts.

Olds was able to use a mild cam and relatively modest axle ratios to fashion a mannered muscle car that still went quite well. Careful suspension tuning helped it handle better than other GM intermediates too. The 4-4-2 was now a legit contender in the muscle-car sweepstakes.

1966 CHEVROLET CHEVELLE SS396

Chevrolet repositioned its Chevelle Super Sport as an all-out performance car for 1966, but in some ways, more turned out to be less. Like other GM intermediates, it was reskinned, though dimensions hardly changed. SS models got a blackout grille and a new hood with nonfunctional vents. With engines of around 400 cubic-inches now obligatory in this game, Chevy made the 396 "big-block" V-8 standard, so all its midsize muscle cars were Chevelle SS396s.

But instead of the 375-horsepower Z-16 396 that debuted midway through the '65 model year, the '66s got detuned 396s rated at 325 horses in base Turbo-Jet guise and 360 ponies in optional L34 form. Nearly a third of SS396 buyers forked over the $105 extra for the L34, but the engine's quarter-mile times in the mid-15s at about 90 mph were pretty ordinary.

So was much the rest of the car, at least compared to the pricey, limited-edition Z-16. Underneath, the '66 SS396 used standard Chevelle brakes and suspension pieces. Chevy claimed there were stiffer springs and shocks—an assertion some testers disputed once they experienced the car's wayward handling and subpar stopping ability. In all fairness though, comfortable seats, tractable engines, sporty styling, and a $2776 base price made the '66 SS396 a great daily driver on the street.

Then in spring, Chevy released the L78 396. This was basically an updated Z-16, but with solid lifters and new exhaust manifolds. With 375 horsepower, the L78 was the 396 that hardcore Chevy street warriors were waiting for.

Nineteen Sixty-Six was the year of the Street Hemi. At Dodge, the new de-tuned version of the 426-cubic-inch race engine was available in the restyled Coronet and the new Coronet-based Charger fastback. Plymouth sold the engine in its related Belvedere and Satellite models.

Actual horsepower was near 500, but Dodge advertised the Street Hemi at 425 ponies on a 10.25:1 compression ratio. The new customer Hemi retained solid lifters, but ran a milder cam for smoother low-rpm running, cast-iron instead of aluminum heads, and a heat chamber so it was able to warm up properly. Engineers also added a choke so the engine could start in cold weather. It also mounted its dual quads inline, rather than on the cross-ram intake manifold. The engine option itself added $1000 to the $2551 base price of a Coronet 440 two-door hardtop.

Hemi cars also received stiffer springs and bigger 11-inch diameter police-grade drum brakes. Still, the nose-heavy Coronet was sloppy in turns and took a long time to stop. Transmission choices were a four-speed manual or TorqueFlite automatic. Around-town fuel economy was in the 10-to-13 mpg range.

None of this was really unusual at the time for a truly hot machine, but here finally was an ultra-supercar that wasn't also burdened with poor drivability. With the Street Hemi, a Coronet was big-league quick—*Car and Driver*'s test car did 0-60 mph in 5.3 seconds and ran the quarter mile in 13.8 seconds at 104 mph. *Motor Trend* called the acceleration "Absolutely shattering."

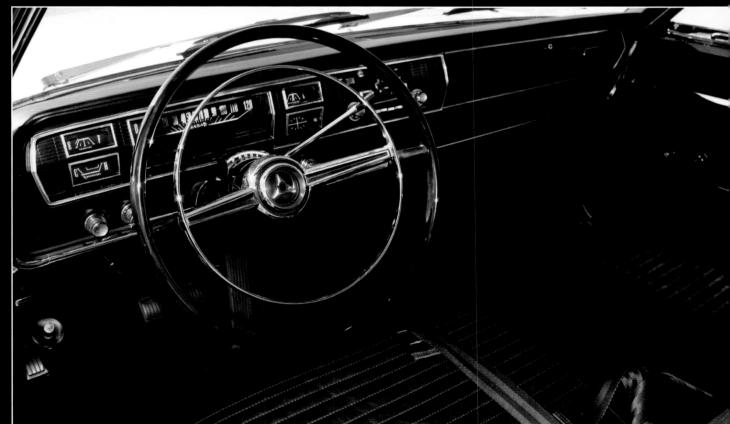

1966 FORD GALAXIE 7-LITRE

For Ford's 1966 full-size cars, the '65 styling was modified, adding flowing "Coke-bottle" rear fenders with a bit of Pontiac flavor. The backlight and long, slender rear pillars of two-door hardtops now had a slight concavity. Taillights became more square, the grille and hood were pushed forward a bit, and rear wheel arches were enlarged slightly, but the balance of the '65 styling remained.

Two new options were power front disc brakes and a 345-horsepower 428-cubic-inch V-8 engine. These two items came together in a new subseries: the Galaxie 500 7-Litre, a sort of super XL that cost about $390 more than a Galaxie 500/XL convertible or hardtop. The model designation referred to the size of the 428 engine in metric terms.

The XL and 7-Litre shared side trim and a diecast grille that was different than the stamped unit on the Galaxie 500. The two models also shared the same all-vinyl interior with bucket seats and center console.

The 428 V-8 was a relatively low-output job with a smaller bore and a longer stroke than the 427, and was designed for smoothness rather than brute power. In standard tune it was rated at 345 horses, and 360 was optional, both with single four-barrel carburetors. Despite its heft, a 7-Litre was actually quite fast, with automatic versions able to accelerate 0-60 mph in about eight seconds.

The market was turning away from full-sized sport models, though. XL orders, which had dropped precipitously in '65, fell to 32,075. Just 11,073 of the 7-Litres were produced. Even these were more luxury liners with a hint of sport.

1966 MERCURY CYCLONE GT

Mercury's first venture into the intermediate field, the 1962-63 Meteor, was not a success. The second try turned out better. For 1966, there was a new intermediate line branded Comet. Previously, Comet was Ford Motor Company's "senior compact" that started out playing big brother to the Ford Falcon.

The Comet faced some big performance guns: Pontiac's GTO, Oldsmobile's 4-4-2, and the Dodge Coronet and Plymouth Belvedere that were now offered with the Street Hemi. Mercury's opening salvo was a weak one.

The Cyclone was back as the performance entry in two-door hardtop and convertible form. The GT option brought a warmed-up 390-cubic-inch V-8 that was rated at 335 horsepower. It also included chrome engine dress-up pieces, a fiberglass hood with fake scoops, and rocker panel striping. Trouble was, the Cyclone GT didn't have enough go for its class—especially at the drags, where it was usually eaten alive.

The Cyclone did turn out to be a dragstrip sensation is 1966 though, just not in street-stock trim. The funny car as we know it today debuted in January 1966. It was "Dyno" Don Nicholson's Eliminator I Comet, the first full "flip-top" fiberglass body on a chromemoly tube frame for a total weight of about 1800 pounds. It ran an injected SOHC 427 cubic-inch V-8 that put out something like 900 horsepower. Ed Schartman ran a similar funny Comet, and he was the only other racer at Nicholson's level in 1966. Both could run 7.80s in the quarter at about 175 mph; other "funny cars" were about a half-second slower.

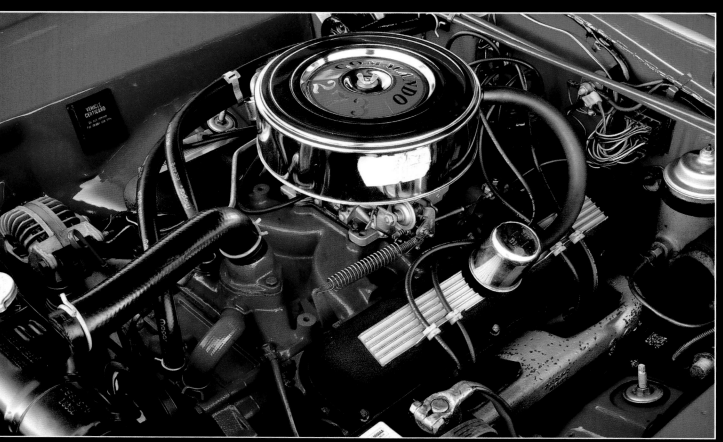

1966 PLYMOUTH BARRACUDA FORMULA S

The 1964 Plymouth Barracuda was announced on Wednesday, April 1, 1964, though it didn't start hitting showrooms in force until May. Just 16 days later, Ford took the wraps off the Mustang in its corporate pavilion at the New York World's Fair. The latter was an instant sales sensation, a vehicle that defined a new market segment: the "ponycar."

Like Ford, Plymouth, too, based its new sporty car on the in-house compact. However, the Barracuda's chief distinction was its fastback roof with a vast rear window; below the beltline it looked much like any of the quarter-million Valiants produced for '64. There was even a Valiant nameplate on the tail panel and a red-and-blue Valiant vee logo in the trim band at the base of the back window.

After production of the 1965 Barracudas began, Plymouth added an optional Formula "S" sports package. It came with a 235-horsepower 273-cubic-inch Commando V-8, rallye suspension, firmer shock absorbers, and a tachometer. The Formula S package cost $258 and addressed the criticisms of reviewers who, after driving the '64 Barracuda, felt the car needed more power and better handling to make it feel as sporty as it looked.

The 1966 models wore altered sheetmetal and a remodeled three-section grille. A further step towards establishing a distinct identity for the Barracuda came in the form of an emblem that depicted its predatory aquatic namesake. Tweaks included newly optional front disc brakes and rear springs with six leaves for Formula S models.

1966 PONTIAC 2+2

1966 PONTIAC 2+2

Pontiac introduced a 2+2 performance version of the full-size Catalina for 1964. Think of it as the GTO's big brother. The 2+2 was elevated to full-series status for 1966, and still came as a two-door hardtop or convertible.

Core styling changes were in line with the rest of Pontiac's big-car line. Up front, there was a new "cat's whiskers" grille and a frenched headlight treatment. Out back, the tail panel adopted hollowed-out end caps and taillamps set in elliptical chrome housings. There were new bumpers front and rear too.

The body sides were largely unchanged, but here 2+2 saw its greatest visual distinction from the Catalina. The tacked-on front fender louvers of '65 were replaced with gill-like simulated brake cooling ducts cut into the rear quarters just behind the door openings. Plus, while the Catalina shifted to a full-length mid-body spear for its exterior bright trim, the 2+2 retained a skeg molding, albeit a thinner one than in 1965.

The 2+2 powertrain lineup went largely unchanged. The standard engine was a four-barrel 421-cubic-inch V-8 rated at 338 horsepower. Two upgrades were on offer, both tri-power 421s. These came with 356 or 376 horses. Three- and four-speed manuals were available, as was the Turbo Hydra-matic 400.

Demand for the 1966 2+2 did not meet expectations, as production dropped to 6383 units—2208 equipped with the manual transmissions and 4175 with the automatic. Due to the sluggish sales, the 2+2 reverted to being a Catalina option package for 1967.

1967 BUICK GS400

Buick's muscle machine stopped living its little lie for 1967, and was better for it. Gone was the 401-cubic-inch V-8 that had masqueraded as a 400. In its place was a genuine 400-cube V-8 (well, actually a 399.748-cubic-inch one), and the swap was marked by a change in name, from Gran Sport to GS400.

Its hood scoops now faced forward, but they remained merely decorative. The dashboard remained unsporting, and though a tachometer was a $47 option, it was mounted too low to read easily. With prices the highest of GM's four muscle intermediates, sales were slow. But for those willing to think in terms of all-around performance, the GS400 delivered.

Like the top version of the 401, the 400 had 10.25:1 compression, hydraulic lifters, and 340 horsepower. But the new engine was of more-modern design, smoother running, higher-revving, and easier to keep in tune. It was even topped off with a futuristic plastic air cleaner.

Helping get the most from the new V-8 was a new optional automatic transmission with three speeds instead of two. Most testers preferred it to the three- or four-speed manuals, despite its extra $237 cost and 58 pounds of weight.

GS400s came as two-door hardtops, pillared coupes, and convertibles, all with the ragtop's stouter frame. Chassis solidity was notable, and with newly standard F70×14 wide-oval tires, handling was among the best in class. Stopping ability was fine too, thanks to power front disc brakes, a new $147 option. Sales continued to languish though, with orders coming in short of 14,000.

1967 CHEVROLET CAMARO Z28

The Sports Car Club of America's Trans American sedan series was the premier racing showcase for pony cars in the late '60s. Obviously, Chevy had to score there to hurt the entrenched Mustang.

Trans Am racers were production-based cars with engines of 305 cubic inches or less. Chevy worked a forged steel version of the 283-cube V-8's crankshaft into its 327 to come up with a 302 cubic-inch V-8. Big-port Corvette heads, solid lifters, a hot cam, a baffled oil pan, and a Holley four-barrel carb were specified. Horsepower was rated at 290.

At least 1000 streetable examples had to be produced, and Chevy's plan was to make the 302 part of a Camaro Regular Production Option Code. So low-key was the effort that the car wasn't advertised, or even mentioned in sales literature. The in-the-know buyer had to order a base six-cylinder Camaro, then scan the order sheet for what turned out to be the most famous RPO in history: Z28.

The package added $400 to the car's $2466 starting tab and included the 302, Chevy's F41 handling suspension, 15-inch tires on Corvette Rally wheels, and quick-ratio manual steering. A Muncie four-speed was the only transmission, and power front disc brakes were a mandatory $100 option.

RPO Z28 was available only on the hardtop coupe and could be combined with the hidden-headlamp Rally Sport option group. There were no Z28 emblems on the car, but the package did include broad racing stripes on the hood and decklid. A rear lip spoiler was a popular option.

1967 CHEVROLET IMPALA SS427

The 1967 full-sized Chevrolets had virtually all new exteriors, designed to suggest a luxurious "big car" look. To many, the new cars looked bulky, especially compared to their lithe 1965 and '66 predecessors. However, in reality, overall length was exactly the same as the 1966 models, and the '67s were less than a half-inch wider.

The 119-inch wheelbase chassis continued with the perimeter frame introduced for the 1965 models. There were still coil springs at all four corners, but numerous detail changes enhanced ride and passenger comfort.

Super Sport models retained black exterior accents. Inside, SS buyers could now choose Strato-bucket seats with a console, or a Strato-back bench with folding center armrest. Per tradition, the SS was only available as a sport coupe or convertible. This was the final year the Impala SS would be a standalone series.

Chevy offered a wide range of engines in the SS, starting with a 250-cubic-inch six with 155 horsepower all the way up to a 385-horsepower 427 V-8. An even more powerful L72 427 with 425 horsepower was available by special order.

There was also a new SS427 performance package. It included the same 427 available throughout the full-size line, and also added stiffer springs and shocks, a front stabilizer bar, and redline tires. Exclusive exterior styling features included a unique domed hood with faux air-intake scoops, blacked-out vertical grille bars, and special emblems. Interestingly, there were no Impala emblems anywhere on the car. Total SS427 production for 1967 was just 2124 examples.

1967 DODGE CHARGER

Plymouth's 1964 Barracuda was America's first modern fastback, beating Ford's '65 Mustang 2+2 to market by about two weeks. Dodge joined the fray for 1966, and then leaped in with muscle other fastbacks could only dream of.

Built on the midsize Coronet body, the Charger added a rather graceless fastback roofline, hidden headlamps, and full-width taillamps. Also part of the deal was a state-of-the-art '60s interior: lots of chrome, four bucket seats (the rears folded down), an optional center console, and full gauges.

One of Charger's missions was to win stock-car races. What could be better than this sleek fastback to put Dodge in the winner's circle? Well, it turned out that the Charger had aerodynamic troubles. On the superspeedways like Daytona, the car's rear wheels tended to lift noticeably—not very desirable for handling stability at speeds approaching 200 mph. Not until a small rear spoiler was added were the Chargers really able to charge.

Rules fights kept the factory-backed Fords on the sidelines in 1966, so Chrysler products ruled NASCAR. Dodge's total of 18 wins was the most of any make, and David Pearson won the driving championship. Richard Petty dominated the '67 season in his Plymouth, but Dodge managed another five wins.

Back to the street. Alterations were minor for the 1967 Charger. Big news was the availability of the 440 Magnum V-8, and a vinyl roof, in black or white, was a new option. Production fell from 1966's 37,344 to 15,788. Only 118 had the mighty Street Hemi, still conservatively rated at 425 horsepower.

1967 PLYMOUTH GTX

There were plenty of fast Plymouths before 1967, but none had the unified performance image pioneered in 1964 by Pontiac's GTO. Plymouth addressed this for '67 with an executive-class hot rod that leaned a bit on the Poncho for its name: GTX.

Based on the good-looking two-door Belvedere hardtop and convertible, the GTX dressed up with a special grille and tail panel, simulated hood scoops, and a chrome gas cap. Twin racing stripes were optional. The cabin was top-of-the-line, with bucket seats, embossed vinyl, and lots of brightwork.

Going fast without a fuss was the GTX's main mission, so it got Mopar's newly fortified 375-horsepower 440 cubic-inch V-8. This was Chrysler's big-car engine improved for high-rpm performance with a revised camshaft and valve-train, and free-flowing intake and exhaust systems.

Mopar's unassailable three-speed TorqueFlite automatic was standard. A four-speed stick was optional and came with some serious stuff, including a larger ring gear, double-breaker distributor, and even an oil-pan windage tray.

Six-leaf rear springs, plus heavy-duty shocks, torsion bars, and ball joints had critics praising the GTX's handling, though most found the optional power steering grossly overassisted.

Some 720 buyers forked over an additional $546 for the GTX's sole engine option, the 425-horsepower 426 Street Hemi. It could run the quarter in the low 13s, but the 440/TorqueFlite combo was its equal in most street tussles.

1967 PONTIAC GTO

Details can mean so much. To their muscle car's pleasing nose, Pontiac designers added simple polished "chain link" grille inserts. At the tail, they resculpted some edges and cleaned up the lamps. Without disturbing the matchless lines of the '66, the stylists created an aesthetic triumph—the 1967 GTO.

There was something fresh behind that gorgeous new grille: The standard engine was now a 400 cubic-inch enlargement of the 389 V-8. Compression was unchanged and the base four-barrel again made 335 horsepower. But taking over the 360-horse slot from the discontinued tri-carb setup was a new four-barrel High Output option. It cost $77 extra and added a higher-lift cam, free-flow exhaust manifolds, and an open-element air cleaner.

For another $263, the HO mill could be fitted with Ram Air. These ultimate GTO V-8s had extra-strong valve springs, a longer-duration cam, and were underrated at 360 horses. The Ram Air package consisted of hardware that opened the otherwise nonfunctional hood scoops, plus a pan that went around the open-element air cleaner and mated to the hood with a foam-rubber skirt. Ram Air was a factory option ordered on 751 cars, but the parts were shipped in the car's trunk for installation by the dealer. Pontiac advised that the car's owner refit the closed-scoop hardware during wet weather.

Hurst-shifted three- and four-speeds were the manual transmission offerings, and the automatic was a newly available three-speed Turbo Hydra-matic. The latter came with a Hurst Dual Gate shifter when the console was ordered.

1968 CHEVROLET EL CAMINO SS396

In a one-year break with tradition, the El Camino was officially part of the 1968 Chevelle lineup. This was the first El Camino that wasn't required to share B-pillar elements and quarter panels with a passenger car, which allowed General Motors truck stylists to create a unique roofline. The cargo box again featured double-wall construction and ample hauling capacity.

Measuring 207 inches overall, the 1968 El Camino was 10 inches longer than its predecessor, yet wheelbase was only up an inch to 116. Chevelle's perimeter frame was specially braced for its truck application, but full-coil suspension was retained, as were standard load-leveling air-booster rear shocks. As on passenger models, drum brakes were standard, front discs optional.

The most exciting '68 development—apart from the sharp new design—was the addition of an "official" SS396 model equipped much like Super Sport Chevelles. Beneath a special hood with "power bulges" lurked a 325-horsepower version of Chevy's 396 V-8. A stronger 350-horse unit was optional, as was GM's three-speed Turbo Hydra-matic transmission.

Other SS-only goodies included a black-accented grille and tailgate—the lower-body perimeter was also finished in black except with optional lower-body stripes. SS emblems graced the grille and tailgate. "Strato" bucket seats and a center console were optional.

El Camino production surpassed 40,000 units for 1968, a first in the model's history. Of the 41,791 produced, only 5190 were SS396 models.

1968 DODGE DART GTS

Dodge's Dart compacts were redone for 1967. Wheelbase stood pat at 111 inches, but there was now enough room under the hood for a big-block V-8 if the situation warranted. Dodge soon filled the available space, and squeezed in a 280-horsepower 383 cubic-inch engine.

The hot Dodges in 1968 were marketed as the "Scat Pack." Dart's member in the bumble-bee-striped fraternity was the GT Sport, usually referred to as the GTS. There were two-door hardtop and convertible versions with buckets and fake hood vents. The GTS was powered by a new standard engine. It was a small-block 340 V-8, an enlargement of the 318. The 383 big-block was still on offer too, but now was rated at an even 300 ponies.

But even that wasn't enough to run with the hottest stocks at the drags. So, the implausible Hemi Dart was concocted along the lines of the earlier Ram Charger intermediates. For a little over $4000, drag racers could buy a stripped Hemi-powered two door, with beefed up drivetrain and suspension, and fiberglass body parts including a scooped hood.

The cars were also outfitted with lightweight window glass, and the side windows had to be raised by pulling on a strap because the window-winder assemblies were left out to save weight. So were the body sealers and sound-deadening insulation. Production was very limited.

Some dealers stuffed 440 big-blocks and Hemis into '68 Darts too. The most famous of these was "Mr. Norm's" Grand-Spaulding Dodge in Chicago.

1968 FORD TORINO GT

For 1968, Ford's Fairlane intermediate retained its previous chassis, but gained all-new styling. Also, the Fairlane name was downplayed in favor of the related but flashier new Torinos, which formed a separate series. There was also a slippery new two-door fastback body style that came in Fairlane 500 and Torino GT flavors.

The Torino GT replaced the Fairlane GT, and came in convertible, hardtop coupe, and racy fastback versions. At introduction, all came with bodyside stripes, styled-steel wheels, all-vinyl upholstery, and a new emissions-friendly 302-cubic-inch small-block V-8. Available power options ranged up to the still-potent 427 with a mighty 390 horsepower.

The 427 was phased out during the year, and for a time, a 335-horsepower 390-cubic-inch big-block was top dog. Eventually the new 335-horsepower 428 Cobra Jet started appearing under Torino hoods. Actual horsepower was un-doubtedly higher than Ford quoted.

The fastbacks were very successful oval-track stock-car racers. Ford captured 20 wins in NASCAR's top series, and David Pearson was the season champion. A.J. Foyt was the USAC champ in a Fairlane.

The new Fairlane/Torino was a real sales champ. Production climbed by more than 50 percent over the 1967 tally, setting a record at over 372,000 cars. Significantly, the most popular single variant was the slick GT fastback with 74,135 sold, and dealers moved more than 32,000 of the Fairlane 500 fastbacks.

ates for 1968. Two-door models now ran a 112-inch wheelbase, three inches shorter than before. Styling was much more youthful and sporty with long-hood/ short-deck profiles, and the windshield wipers were now hidden. Bodysides billowed out in an arc, a distinct departure from the flatter sides of the 1964-67 A-bodies, and roofs blended smoothly into the rear quarters. Two-door hardtops and pillared coupes featured a stylish sloping roofline.

From this core shared with other GM divisions, Oldsmobile fashioned a distinct identity for its version. Front styling carried over 1967's widely spaced quad headlamps with turn-indicator lamps set between each pair. The grille was aggressively vee'd and, on most models, made up of bold vertical bars. Muscular fender flares were clearly inspired by the personal-luxury Olds Toronado.

Base models were the modestly trimmed F-85s. The extensive Cutlass clan formed the bulk of the lineup. All two-door models were called "Cutlass S," and came as a pillared "Sports Coupe," a hardtop, and a convertible. The 4-4-2 muscle cars were elevated to separate-series status for '68.

Buyers looking for a "goer" without raising the suspicions of their insurance agent could choose a new late-arriving W-31 option. It was available on the F-85 coupe and Cutlass S coupe and hardtop, and it added a Force-Air 350-cubic-inch V-8 with a healthy 325 horsepower. It was only available with manual transmission, and was marked by small "Ram Rod" badges.

1968 PLYMOUTH GTX

With the hot new Road Runner anchoring the lower rungs, a familiar name returned to top off Plymouth's mid-size muscle ladder. For its second season, the GTX used the same redesigned Belvedere platform as the Road Runner.

In keeping with its upscale mission, the GTX featured two-door hardtop and convertible body styles. The '68 Road Runner started with a pillared coupe and didn't come as a ragtop.

GTX carried over its '67 powertrains. The 375-horsepower 440-cubic-inch V-8 was standard, with the take-no-prisoners 425-horse 426 Hemi the sole engine option. TorqueFlite automatic, a $206 extra on the Road Runner, was standard on the GTX, and the four-speed manual was a no-cost choice. Both had similar suspension upgrades and wide-oval rubber; front disc brakes and a limited-slip diff were shared options. Nonfunctional hood vents were common to both.

While even a loaded Road Runner looked pretty plain on the outside, the GTX dressed its part with standard chrome wheel-lip moldings, tail-panel brightwork, and double side stripes. And where the Road Runner started with a fleet-grade interior, the GTX came with the well-appointed Sport Satellite cabin featuring shiny details and fake woodgrain. The differences showed in base prices: $3355 for the GTX hardtop, $3034 for the Road Runner coupe.

Die-hard racers types still loved the Hemi, but just 450 GTXs were ordered with the $564 option. The 440 was easier to keep in tune, and unlike the Hemi churned out a surplus of low-end torque for unparalleled response on the street.

1968 SHELBY GT-500KR

Carroll Shelby's Mustangs returned for 1968 with fastback and convertible body styles in small-block GT-350 guise and big-inch GT-500 trim. Though the Shelby Mustangs still looked quite a bit wilder than Ford's own ponies, in reality they were becoming less special.

For '68 Ford shifted Shelby production from Carroll Shelby's Los Angeles, California, plant to Livonia, Michigan, which wasn't far from Dearborn. There, contractor A.O. Smith carried out the conversions.

All '68 Shelby Mustangs wore a revised nose with a larger, more aggressive grille opening in a new fiberglass front fascia. The redesigned hood added a pair of air scoops at the leading edge. As before, the hood and bodyside scoops were functional, as were those on the fastback's roof.

A handful of Shelby convertibles had been built to order in earlier years, but for 1968 the ragtop was officially cataloged. Convertibles had a padded roll bar, and all the '68s gained 1965 Thunderbird sequential taillights.

Midyear, GT-500s added the initials KR—for King of the Road—and gained a new "Cobra Jet" version of the Ford 428-cubic-inch V-8. Medium-riser heads and a 735cfm Holley four-barrel were part of the deal. The engine was advertised at 335 horsepower, but in reality, the CJ produced something like 400. The 335-horsepower claim was even more puzzling when you consider the CJ replaced a 360-horsepower 428 Police Interceptor.

A GT-500KR convertible started at a princely $4594. Only 318 were built.

1969 AMC HURST SC/RAMBLER

Laugh if you will, but the AMC Hurst SC/Rambler could blow the doors off some pedigreed muscle cars. Too bad AMC had to compensate for its slim advertising budget by making a billboard of the car itself. Having dipped into the performance market with the '68 AMX and Javelin pony cars, Detroit's No. 4 automaker decided to expand into the budget-muscle arena with—don't snicker—a compact Rambler Rogue hardtop.

Directed by Hurst Performance Research Inc., the project followed the simplest hot-rod cannon: stuff in the biggest available V-8. In AMC's case, that was the AMX's 315-horsepower 390-cubic-inch four-barrel. A Borg-Warner four-speed with a Hurst shifter and a 3.54:1 limited-slip diff completed the drivetrain.

Heavy-duty shocks, anti-sway bar, and anti-hop rear links fortified the suspension. E70×14 Polyglas tires and AMC's optional heavy-duty brakes with front discs were included. Instrumentation was standard Rogue with the exception of a Sun 8000-rpm tach strapped to the steering column.

All SC/Ramblers started as appliance white hardtops with blue-accented mags, racing mirrors, blackout grille and tail panel, Hurst badging, and a real ram-air hood scoop. The car debuted midyear as the SC/Rambler-Hurst, but almost everybody simply called it the Scrambler.

Only 1512 were built. About 1012 Scramblers went full "Yankee Doodle," with broad red bodysides, wild hood graphics, and a fat blue dorsal stripe. The rest were like the car seen here with simple rocker-panel striping.

1969 AMC JAVELIN SST

After Ford's runaway success with the Mustang in 1964, other carmakers went galloping to their drawing boards to bring out their own sporty compacts. American Motors was one of the last to enter what became known as the ponycar field. Its contender was the 1968 Javelin. Styled by Dick Teague, the two-door fastback sat on a 109-inch wheelbase, and was sold in basic and fancier SST trim. Six-cylinder and V-8 power was on offer. Later in '68, the Javelin served as the base for the shorter two-seat AMX.

AMC billed it as a "full 4-passenger sporty car," and it did indeed have a roomier interior than most of its competitors. Styling was beautifully clean and uncluttered in the long-hood/short-deck ponycar idiom, its smoothness accentuated by flush door handles, ventless side glass, and sweeping "C" pillars. The interior featured standard front bucket seats and deeply recessed full instrumentation in a padded ABS plastic panel.

The 1969 Javelin was much the same as the '68 offering inside and out. The available "Go" package added fake hood scoops, and a "Big Bad" option package became available for the top-line SST mid-year. This featured the choice of three bold paint colors, color-keyed urethane bumpers, a roof-mounted spoiler, stripes, and other trick appearance gear.

The top engine choice was a 315-horsepower version of AMC's 390-cubic-inch V-8. It was derived from AMC's 343 mill, but it carried a stronger block, forged connecting rods and crank, and bigger bearings.

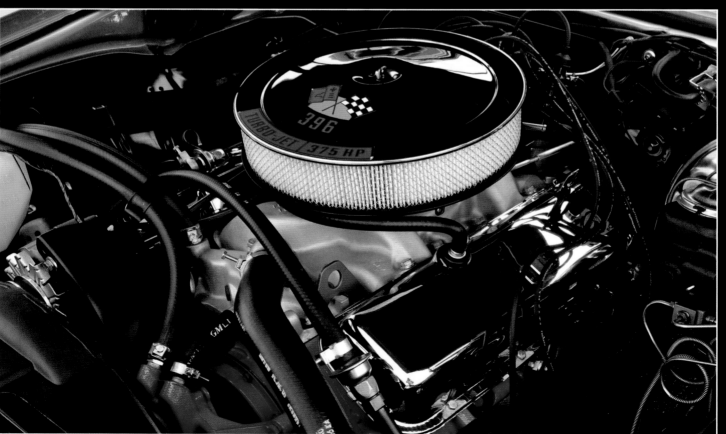

1969 CHEVROLET CAMARO SS/RS

The 1969 Camaros saw extensive alterations—a good thing, as they would be sold into early 1970, owing to delays in bringing out the all-new second-generation design. A deft below-the-belt reskin of the 1967-68 bodyshell yielded a squarer, huskier appearance announced by a vee'd eggcrate grille. Sculpted "speed streaks" added visual interest above the wheel arches, the tail was re-shaped, and there were the expected adjustments to exterior trim and taillights. A revamped dashboard put the two main circular gauges into square surrounds and brought the climate and radio controls closer to the driver.

Mechanical upgrades affecting all '69 Camaros began with all-wheel-disc brakes as an across-the-board regular-production option (RPO). Also the Power-glide automatic was finally retired in favor of the modern Turbo Hydra-matic.

Rally Sport models retained hidden headlamps, but three glass "ribs" allowed some light to shine through the covers should they fail to retract. A damage-resistant body-color front bumper was a new Camaro option.

Super Sport models came with a 300-horsepower 350 V-8. Beyond that, the buyer could order a 396 "big-block" V-8 with at least 325 horsepower. The top regular-production L78 version was good for 375 horses and 415 lb-ft of torque. In this Olympic Gold SS/RS coupe, the L78 is backed by a Muncie M21 four-speed transmission and a Positraction 12-bolt rear end with a 3.55:1 gear. The Muncie picked up Hurst linkage for '69 too. Total 1969 Camaro production was better than 240,000 units.

1969 CHEVROLET YENKO/SC CHEVELLE

By using Chevrolet's Central Office Production Order (COPO) system, Yenko Chevrolet in Pennsylvania and a few other high-performance dealers were able to circumvent GM's ban on engines over 400 cubic inches in midsize cars. The cubic-inch-lid was lifted for 1970, so COPO Chevelles were only built in 1969.

As in the COPO Camaros, the solid-lifter iron-block-and-head 427-cubic-inch L72 engine used an aluminum intake manifold and a Holley four-barrel. Chevy rated it at 425 horsepower.

All COPO Chevelles had front disc brakes and a 12-bolt Positraction rear axle with 4.10:1 gears. There was also a heavy-duty suspension, and Chevelle's strongest regular four-speed or the Rock Crusher manual were available, as was a fortified Turbo 400 Hydra-matic.

None of the 323 COPO Chevelles built were Super Sports. Instead, they were base coupes with a COPO option package that ran about $860, including $533 for the L72. Yenko put his trademark dress-ups on the 99 cars he ordered, but the balance went to other dealers and looked deceptively docile.

From the SS they borrowed a black tail panel, hood bulges, side stripes, and chrome exhaust tips. However, there was no performance ID on the body. The emblem-free L72 could pass for an aluminum-manifold 396. And the cabin was plain Malibu, though a few SS steering wheels were fitted. Even the standard rally wheels looked similar to those on the base Malibu, though in reality they were larger 15-inch units.

1969 CHEVROLET IMPALA SS

The largest Chevrolets moved into 1969 with an all-new exterior appearance, and the fresh styling further disguised that these cars were built on an aging basic structure and chassis that originated with Chevy's 1965 models. Prominent bodyside bulges put none-too-subtle emphasis on the more elliptical wheel openings. The front bumper design surrounded the grille opening, allowing designers to stretch the hood from upper bumper to windshield. Even with new flush-mounted bumper ends, overall length was up by as much as 1.2 inches— these were the longest Chevrolets yet.

Inside, a revised instrument panel put controls and gauges more directly in the driver's view. Astro Ventilation was now standard, so all 1969 models had single-pane door glass.

Chevy abandoned Impala's slope-roof two-door hardtop design for 1969. It was replaced with a new Impala sport coupe that used a more angular look similar to the Bel Air and Biscayne two-door sedans. Uplevel Impala Custom and Caprice coupes featured a new, even more squared formal roofline, with a fresh concave rear window treatment.

The Impala Super Sport put in its last appearance in 1969, and would remain retired until 1994. For '69 the SS was a $422 option package for hardtops and convertibles, and was only available with the 427 big block in 335- and 390-horsepower versions. There was also a "secret" 425-horse tune that wasn't officially cataloged. SS production was only 2455 units.

1969 DODGE CHARGER 500

"Win on Sunday, Sell on Monday" was a Detroit mantra in the 1960s. It was truest of NASCAR performance, and the all-out war between Chrysler and Ford for superspeedway supremacy produced some of the most outlandish machines of the muscle age.

Dodge's '68 Charger was an aerodynamic washout on the nation's 190-mph high-banked ovals. To reduce drag, Mopar engineers plugged the nose cavity with a flush-mounted Coronet grille. They quelled lift by flush-mounting a rear window over the recessed backlight. The new racer was called the Charger 500, and 392 similarly modified production cars were built so it would be eligible to be raced in NASCAR. They were basically Charger R/Ts with Charger 500 metalwork. Fifty-two were equipped with the still-mighty 426-cubic-inch Hemi, and the remaining 340 were fitted with the 440.

Racing Charger 500s captured 18 NASCAR victories in 1969. Trouble was, Ford's droop-nosed aero warriors won 30. The Mopar engineers headed back to the wind tunnel, and they emerged with the Charger Daytona. Instead of the 500's flush nose, the Daytona wore a pointed 18-inch extension that reduced drag and enhanced downforce. The Charger 500's flush rear glass was retained, but rear-end lift was eliminated by mounting a horizontal tail stabilizer on tall vertical extensions. Again, street-going versions had to be built, and approximately 505 were. In NASCAR trim, the Daytona was faster than a 500, but it arrived too late in the season to beat Ford.

1969 DODGE SUPER BEE

Dodge continued to fine-tune its budget Super Bee muscle car for 1969. Styling was touched up with a new grille and taillamps. Newly optional was the Ramcharger fresh-air induction package that came with a two-scoop hood.

The standard Super Bee mill continued to be the 383-cubic-inch V-8 with 335 horsepower. At the beginning of the year, the only engine upgrade was the mighty 426 Hemi with its 425 ponies.

Midyear, Chrysler engineers cooked up a new Super Bee Six Pack model. It packed Mopar's fine 440-cubic-inch V-8 with three Holley two-barrels on an aluminum Edelbrock Hi-Riser intake. Hemi valve springs, a hotter cam, magnafluxed connecting rods, and other fortifications helped add up to 390 horsepower.

The Six Pack name was broadcast on the sides of one of the wilder hoods in muscledom. Its scoop lacked any kind of filter or mechanism to keep out foreign elements—though it did have rain drain tubes. With its matte-black finish and NASCAR-style tie-down pins, the fiberglass hood clearly communicated that this car meant business. The message was reinforced by standard steel wheels unadorned except for chrome lug nuts.

No Mopar mill was as all-out fast as the Hemi, but the 440 could hang with one until 70 mph or so, and the deep-breathing Six Pack added a near-Hemi top end. Dodge's Six Pack cost $463, about $500 less than a Hemi.

The base Coronet Super Bee pillared coupe started at $3076 in 1969, while a hardtop priced from $3138. Production came to 27,846 units.

1969 FORD MUSTANG BOSS 302

The Ford Mustang was restyled for 1969, gaining 3.8 inches of body length—all ahead of the front wheels—and about 140 pounds of curb weight. Like the Camaro Z28, the Boss 302 was built as a Trans Am road-racing qualifier. Its heart was Ford's 302-cubic-inch V-8 treated to the high-performance, big-port cylinder heads being readied for the famous Cleveland 351. The Boss's solid-lifter small-block used the biggest carb employed by Ford, a 780-cfm Holley four-barrel, and was underrated at the same 290 horsepower as the Z28's 302.

A Hurst-shifted four speed and 3.50:1 gears were standard; 3.91:1 and Detroit Locker 4.30:1 cogs were optional. Underneath were racing inspired suspension tweaks, quicker steering, meaty Polyglas F60×15 boots, and power-assisted front disc brakes.

Aerodynamics influenced the Boss's exterior. Mustang's phony fender vents were smoothly enclosed and a front spoiler was fitted; a rear air foil and back-light blinds were optional. Blackout trim and stripes finished the look.

Ford built 1628 Boss 302s for 1969, then followed that up with 7013 more for '70, when quad headlamps were traded for double units flanked by fake air intakes, a "shaker" hood was made available, and the engine got smaller intake valves and a 6000-rpm rev limiter.

In Trans Am, racing Boss 302s retook the 1970 crown from Chevrolet. The street versions were not always as fast as a 302-powered Camaro Z28, but the Mustangs had more cornering power and a less-peaky, more flexible engine.

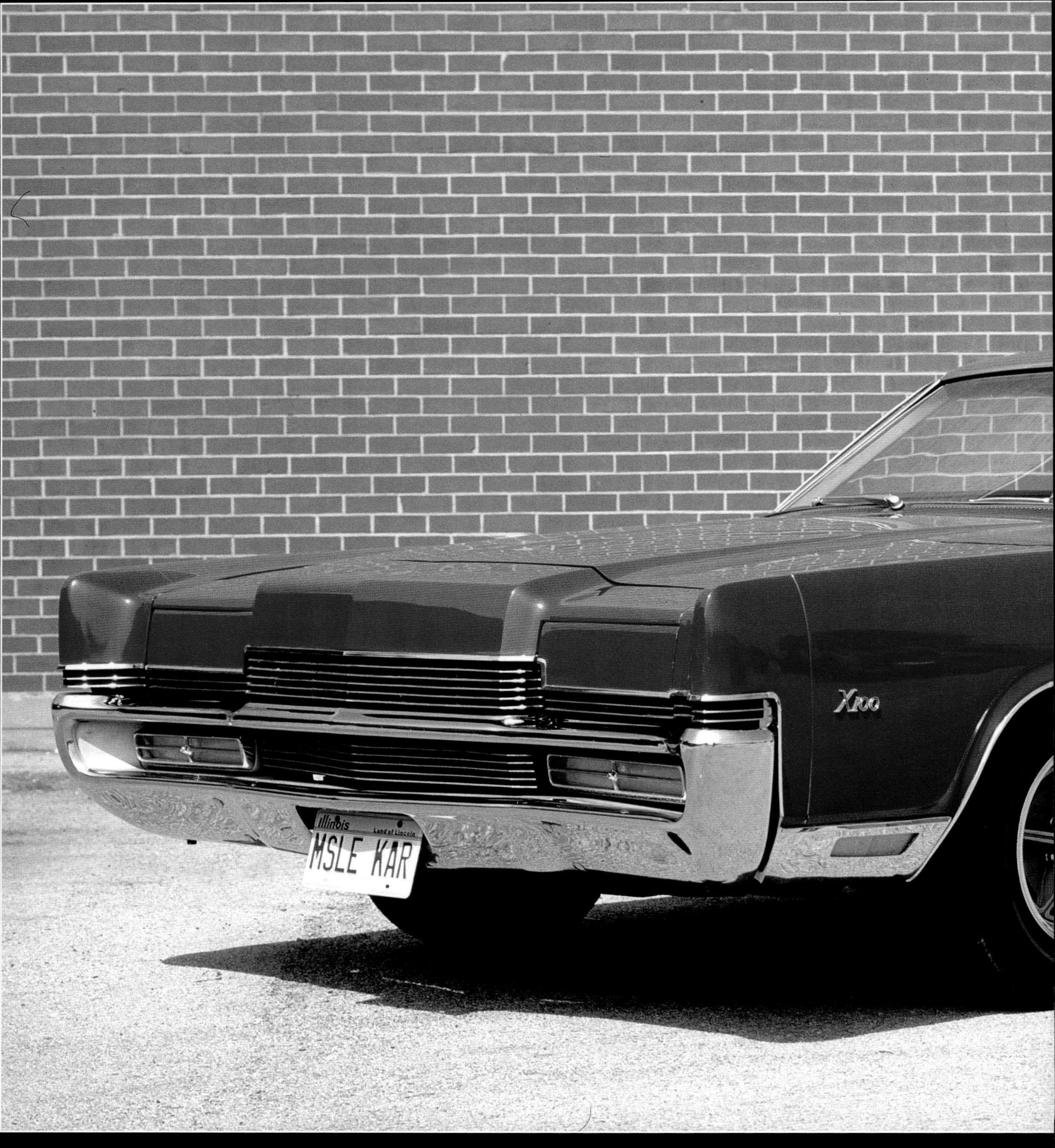
X100
Illinois
Land of Lincoln
MSLE KAR

1969 MERCURY MARAUDER X-100

One idea that had not completely escaped the marketing mavens at Mercury was the full-sized performance car. In 1969, the typical muscle car was a mightily enhanced intermediate like Mercury's Montego-based Cyclone. However, these big-engined midsizers had been preceded in the early Sixties by a slew of high-performance fullsize hardtops and convertibles. Even at the end of the decade, there were still some buyers who liked a full-size powerhouse for the road. Thus, the Marauder was reborn.

The label had been associated with Mercury since 1958, and it had resurfaced in mid 1963 to represent the sleek slopeback roof offered on Monterey two-door hardtops. For 1969 though, the Marauder was a series unto itself, and was a marriage of several models into one package. Frontal styling was shared with the Marquis, and the base interior was identical to that in the Monterey. At the same time, Marauder rode the 121-inch Ford wheelbase, and it borrowed key elements like a tunnel-back roof and doors from the Ford XL.

As good as all this was, the Marauder begged to be dressed up, which is where the $4091 X-100 version came in. It added styled aluminum wheels, fender skirts, and a decklid and backlight area done in a "Sports-tone matte finish."

While the X-100 was a relatively hot looker, it what was underhood that really made the package. Sporting 429 cubic inches and an advertised 360 horsepower and 480 pound-feet of torque, the four-barrel-fed engine could push the big Marauder X-100 to a top speed of 125 mph.

1969 OLDSMOBILE 4-4-2

Oldsmobile's 4-4-2 was back with few changes for 1969. Frontal styling was new this year with headlamps in close-together pairs, a divided grille, and a new hood with a central "tooth" that hung down to mirror a raised portion of the redesigned front bumper. Rear styling was especially handsome with vertical tail lamp/back-up light units set into notches in the trunklid and rear bumper.

Like their Cutlass siblings, the 4-4-2 hardtops and convertibles lost their vent windows; GM's new "Flo-Thru" ventilation system was engineered to do away with the need for ventipanes. A woodgrain band with the look of burled elm stretched across the instrument panel.

The 4-4-2's 400-cubic-inch V-8 was rated at 350 horsepower with the three- or four-speed manual transmissions, and 325 with the Turbo Hydra-matic. The blueprinted W-30 version returned and with standard Force Air was rated at 360 horsepower. The new W-32 package combined the 350-horse motor with the automatic transmission.

The division launched its memorably wacky "Dr. Oldsmobile" advertising campaign this year, which featured a fictitious mad scientist with a silent-movie moustache and baggy white lab coat concocting potent "W-Machines" with the help of a band of ghoulish sidekicks.

Production slipped to 26,357, including 4295 convertibles. The pillared 4-4-2 Sports Coupe had a base price of $3141 and was picked by only 2475 buyers. The hardtop priced from $3204, while the convertible started at $3395.

Experimental cars are among the rarest and most treasured automobiles. Even rarer is a surviving experimental engine—in this case a powerplant known as the "Ball Stud Hemi" (BSH). Making the tale of the BSH even more special is the home of the only known remaining example: within one of the limited numbe of 1969 Plymouth Barracudas originally equipped with a 440 Magnum V-8. This car was once owned by Tom Hoover, known as the father of the 426 Hemi.

The term "ball stud" refers to the pivot arrangement used for the engine's rocker-arm fulcrums. The ball-stud rocker setup was simpler than that of the 426 Hemi's dual rocker shafts, support stands, and immense rocker arms.

Chrysler's hemispherical-head V-8s have retained a magical aura with collectors—especially the 426-cubic-inch version introduced in 1964. For performance enthusiasts, there could never be a better internal-combustion engine. However, Hoover and his team of engineers designed a better one and management nearly put it into production.

Intended for the Seventies and beyond, it was to have clean-burning combustion, greater high-performance potential than the 426 Hemi, reduced production costs, lighter weight, and other benefits. Using the BSH design, displacements were planned at 400, 444, and possibly even 481 cubic inches or more. However, due to uncertainty about federal air-quality regulations, corporate financial difficulties, and other reasons, the program was terminated shortly before production was set to begin.

1969 PLYMOUTH ROAD RUNNER

With the Road Runner accounting for 35 percent of its midsize-car sales, Plymouth didn't tamper much with the winning formula as set out in the 1968 original. A convertible joined the pillared coupe and hardtop, the grille and tail-lamps were revised, and the cartoon-bird insignia were now in full color. Road Runner's budget-bomb vibe changed with new options like a center console, front buckets, and power windows. Five new extra-cost rear-axle packages allowed gear ratios up to 4.10:1.

The 335-horsepower 383-cubic-inch V-8 returned as standard, with the 425-horse 426 Hemi again the top engine option. The base 383 could still deliver sub-15-second ETs in the quarter. Midyear, buyers got a third choice—the same triple-two-barrel 440 V-8 that debuted in the '69 Dodge Super Bee. Here at Plymouth it was called the "440+6" and it came with a big-scoop, lift-off fiberglass hood, Hurst shifter, and a 4.10:1 Sure-Grip. The 390-horsepower 440+6 provided Hemi-style acceleration for about half the price premium.

Plymouth's new "Coyote Duster" cool-air induction system was standard with the Hemi and optional for the 383. The driver could open vents in the standard hood slots to direct outside air through the underhood ducting.

Road Runner production peaked at 84,420, nearly doubling the 1968 tally. This broke down into 33,743 pillared coupes, 48,549 hardtops and 2128 of the new-for-1969 convertibles. Hemis were installed in 788 Road Runners, including just 10 of the ragtops.

TRANS AM

1969 PONTIAC FIREBIRD TRANS AM

In March 1969, the Firebird Trans Am quietly slipped into Pontiac's lineup. It was an inauspicious beginning for a car that would soon become Pontiac's performance flagship.

Officially dubbed the Trans Am Performance and Appearance Package, the $725 option was launched with little fanfare or advertising and was ordered on just 697 Firebird coupes and eight convertibles. Its name came from the popular Trans American road-racing series, though the car never actually competed in Trans Am racing.

Its base engine was the Firebird 400 HO's 335-horsepower 400-cubic-inch V-8, but with standard Ram Air induction. It came to be known as Ram Air III. The only alternative was the Ram Air IV version. Ordered on only 55 Trans Am coupes, Ram Air IV had a longer-duration cam and 345 horsepower. The base mill came with a three-speed stick and 3.55:1 gears, while the Ram Air IV had a four-speed and 3.90:1 cogs. Both were available with an optional automatic transmission. A heavy-duty suspension with a one-inch-diameter front stabilizer bar, Polyglas F70×14s on seven-inch rims, and a special high-effort variable ratio power steering were standard.

All Trans Ams wore Polar White paint with blue racing stripes and tail panel. The hood, a Trans Am exclusive, had functional air inlets. Rear-facing fender scoops covered fist-sized holes designed to vent the engine bay, and a 60-inch air foil spanned the rear deck. A hood-mounted tach cost an extra $85.

1969 PONTIAC GTO

"The Great One" received minor styling updates for 1969 that included an eggcrate-style grille, revised front parking lamps, and a new rear bumper. Vent windows were deleted.

The GTO also had a whimsical new performance model for '69. Pontiac added op-art decals, a rear spoiler, and a 366-horsepower Ram Air III 400 cubic-inch engine to create The Judge, a $332 option package on the GTO. The car's name was a sly pop-culture reference—"Here come da Judge" was a recurring catch-phrase on the popular TV show *Laugh-In*.

The first 5000 Judges were painted Carousel Red (a bright shade of orange) but other colors were offered. The 370-horsepower Ram Air IV was a $390 option. Restless at idle, weak below 3000 rpm, this edition of the 400 was a pain to drive on the street and a challenge to launch on the strip, but it was a weapon in the hands of a skilled driver.

The most famous Pontiac performance dealership of the Sixties was Ace Wilson's Royal Pontiac in Royal Oak, Michigan. The dealership fielded several Pontiac drag cars and offered hopped-up "Royal Bobcat" Pontiacs throughout the decade. The blue-and-white GTO shown here is a one-of-a-kind factory test car that was fitted with an experimental 400-cubic-inch Ram Air V engine that put out about 500 horsepower, but never actually saw production.

GTO's hood-mounted tach was an extra-cost option that was something of a Pontiac staple. It was a cool-looking piece, but was often hard to read.

1970 AMC REBEL MACHINE

There exists in the American Motors archives a photo of a most sinister-looking muscle car. It's a black midsize coupe with authoritative black wheels and fat tires. No stripes, no scoops, no spoilers. Its body rakes forward in an aggressive, street-fighting stance. On the fender is a decal. It shows two gears chewing out the name of this macho prototype: "The Machine."

The photo is dated June 1968, and the car is a '69 Rebel. AMC's high-performance sedan efforts for '69 were focused on the Rogue-based Hurst SC/Rambler, a brashly decorated compact as overstated as the black Rebel concept was understated. The SC/Rambler didn't survive into 1970, but The Machine did.

It did not appear as the malevolent rebel promised by the prototype, but a red, white, and blue jukebox of a car, clearly in the spirit of the SC/Rambler.

Luckily The Machine was a pretty good performer. Like the Scrambler, it used the AMX's ram-air 390-cubic-inch V-8, but it was newly souped up to 340 horsepower. In its journey from concept to reality, The Machine gained a big hood scoop that served the engine via a vacuum-controlled butterfly valve. A Hurst-shifted four-speed was standard. AMC's limited-slip diff was a $43 option, with a genuine Detroit Locker and ratios up to 5.00:1 available.

The Machine turned out to be a one-year-only model, and after building the first 1000 or so, AMC began offering it sans stripes and in any color. It wasn't the menacing machine of that '68 photo, but buyers could at least get the steak without quite so much sizzle.

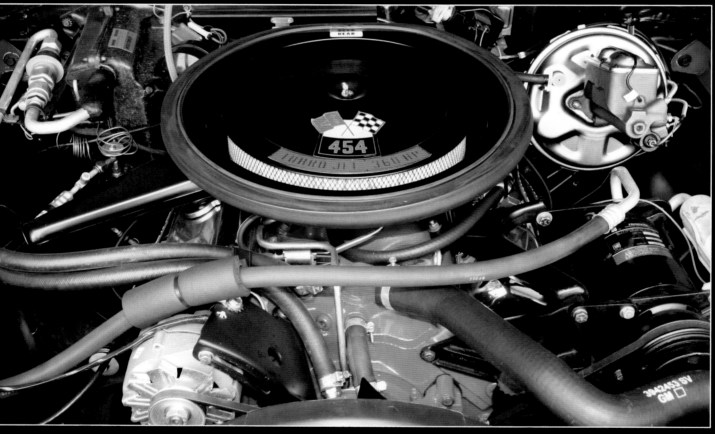

1970 CHEVROLET CHEVELLE SS454

The age of muscle peaked in 1970 and Chevrolet's Chevelle was there to herald its ascent. When GM lifted its displacement ban on midsize cars, Pontiac, Olds, and Buick responded with 455-cubic-inch mills with up to 370 horsepower. Chevy's retort was a 454-cube big-block V-8 that started at 360 horsepower and ended at a barbaric 450. This was muscle's summit.

The wrapper was a restyled Chevelle that again presented the Super Sport as an option package for two-door hardtops and convertibles. As the SS396, it cost $446 and came with a 350-horsepower 402-cube V-8, power front discs, F41 suspension, Polyglas tires, and a domed hood. Fat dorsal stripes were optional, but were included with the new $147 cowl-induction hood.

The new SS454 package cost $503 and included a 360-horse hydraulic-lifter 454 called the LS5. Then there was the LS6. This was the take-no-prisoners 454, with a 800-cfm Holley four-barrel on an aluminum intake, 11.25:1 compression, solid lifters, four-bolt mains, forged steel crank and rods, forged aluminum pistons, and deep-grove accessory pulleys. No production engine of the classic muscle era ever had a higher factory horsepower rating. With mandatory options—including either the Rock Crusher four-speed manual or special Turbo 400 automatic—total cost for an LS6 was more than $1000.

The SS Chevelle had a handsome new dash, and on the road, exhibited far more poise than its weight and size would suggest. But the LS6 made it a superstar. Sub-14-second ETs at over 100 mph were routine.

1970 DODGE CHALLENGER R/T

It took Chrysler six long years to develop a true pony car, and by time the 1970 Dodge Challenger was introduced, it was hard to do anything really new with the formula. Offering an astonishing range of engine choices, from a docile slant six to the earthshaking Hemi, was Dodge's way of getting attention.

Challenger used the same unibody platform as Plymouth's new Barracuda, but its wheelbase was two inches longer. It was sold in hardtop and convertible form, with performance versions wearing the familiar R/T label. Standard R/T power came from the 335-horsepower 383 V-8. Two 440s were offered, a four-barrel Magnum with 375 horsepower and the tri-carb Six Pack with 390. The 425-horse 426 Hemi cost $1228 with the required heavy-duty equipment.

The 440 and Hemi came standard with TorqueFlite automatic. Ordering the four-speed brought a pistol-grip Hurst shifter and a Dana 60 rear axle. All R/Ts got a beefed suspension, and 440 and Hemi cars wore 15-inch 60-series tires, though such essentials as power steering and front disc brakes were optional.

The R/T's standard hood had two scoops that were open but didn't feed directly to the air cleaner. A $97 option was the shaker scoop, which mounted directly to the air cleaner and protruded through an opening in the hood. Full gauges, including a tach, were standard.

Everyday road manners were composed, but the car felt bulky for its size. Hemis were quickest, but not enough to justify the price premium over the next most potent iteration, the 440 Six Pack.

1970 DODGE SUPER BEE

The Super Bee was Dodge's version of Plymouth's popular Road Runner. The Road Runner had proved that a muscle car with a hot engine but no unneeded luxuries to inflate the price or add weight could be a big seller.

Dodge based the Super Bee on its midsize Coronet. An extensive facelift was approved for the 1970 Coronets, most obviously highlighted by an unusual—and controversial—double-delta loop bumper up front. Each loop housed a pair of headlamps and vertical grille bars. The new hood had a dual-inlet power bulge. Optional Ramcharger air induction used a different hood design with two widely spaced scoops. At the rear, horizontally split taillamps recalled the look of the new front bumper/grille units. Side stripes joined the traditional bee-tail graphics. Though the wheelbase held steady at 117 inches, the styling changes added more than three inches to the overall length of the 1970 models.

The standard engine was a 383-cubic-inch V-8 that in 1970 put out 335 horsepower. The only engine options were good ones. The 440 Six Pack was rated at 390 horsepower, and the seldom-ordered 426 Street Hemi was still rated at 425 ponies.

For 1970, Super Bee production ended up totalling 14,254 units. The base pillared coupe started at $3012, while hardtops priced from $3074. The more-expensive but better-trimmed Coronet R/Ts were caught between the budget Super Bees and the costlier but more spectacular-looking Charger R/Ts. It was not a good place to be, and Coronet R/T sales fell to 2408 units for 1970.

1970 FORD MUSTANG BOSS 429

Muscle fans thought the Boss 429 would be the Mustang that could finally rival the best of the Corvettes. They were disappointed when it wasn't. But Ford never intended the Boss 429 as a street dominator, or as any kind of a drag-racing threat. This gap between expectation and intent dimmed the glow of an extraordinary machine.

The Boss 429 was born of Ford's need to qualify 500 examples of its new racing engine for NASCAR. But instead of putting production units in the midsize Torinos it ran in stock-car racing, Ford offered the engines in its restyled Mustang fastback. It was a serious mill: four-bolt mains, a forged steel crankshaft, and big-port, staggered-valve aluminum heads with crescent-shaped combustion chambers. A Holley four-barrel with ram air, an aluminum high-riser, and header-type exhaust manifolds completed the engine, which retailed for $1200. Mandatory options included a four-speed and a 3.91:1 Traction-Lok. An oil cooler, trunk-mounted battery, beefed suspension, Polyglas F60×15s, quicker power steering, and power front discs rounded out the functional hardware.

Boss 429s used Mustang's plushest interior decor and a 8000-rpm tach. They were refreshingly clean outside, with simple decals, hood scoop, front spoiler, and Magnum 500 wheels. But the Boss 429 was the costliest non-Shelby Mustang, and quarter-mile performance fell short of other big-block specialty cars. Ford built 1356 Boss 429 Mustangs and two Mercury Cougars for 1969 and '70 before retiring a car whose promise and purpose never really meshed.

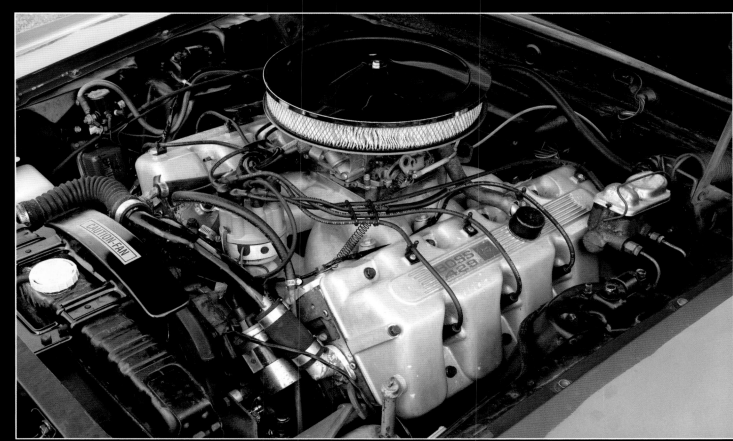

1970 FORD RANCHERO GT

Ford's car-based Ranchero half-ton pickups debuted back in 1957. For 1960, Ford abandoned the full-size-car chassis and adopted the unibody design used by the new compact Falcon. When Falcon switched to larger bodies in 1966, Ranchero followed suit. The top engine was a 225-horsepower 289 V-8.

The 1967 models were similar, but Ranchero now wore Fairlane front sheet-metal rather than the Falcon's. The 390 V-8 with up to 320 horsepower was newly optional. Then for 1968, Ranchero was redesigned along the lines of Ford's midsize-car line. During the year, the mighty 428 Cobra Jet arrived.

The all-new styling theme for the 1970 Torinos again translated to new looks for the Ranchero. Pointed front fender tips, a sharp full-length midbody crease, and an eggcrate grille were key elements of the design, though hidden headlamps were an extra-cost option.

Base, 500, and GT Rancheros were continued, and they were joined by a new Squire that was generously decked out in simulated wood trim. Equipment on the sporty GTs included color-keyed Laser stripes on the bodysides and tailgate, and a "sport-scoop" hood. Buckets and a Hurst-stirred 4-speed were optional.

A trio of 429-cubic-inch V-8s now topped the engine roster in place of the previous 390- and 428-cube mills. The Thunder Jet was rated at 360 horsepower, while the Cobra version was good for 370 ponies and came with a performance handling package. A Cobra Jet could also be ordered, and it started with the Cobra engine and added Ram Air with a pop-through "shaker" hood scoop.

1970 FORD TORINO GT

All-new styling "shaped by the wind" marked the 1970 midsize Fords. Wheelbases grew an inch—to 114 on wagons and 117 inches on the other body styles. Width spread by two inches, overall length grew by four. The interiors were redone, trim was upgraded, and comfort and convenience options proliferated. Basic engineering was untouched.

The GT convertible and "Sportsroof" fastback hardtop and the Cobra fastback remained the hottest members of this clan. The latter continued as Ford's budget muscle car, with a standard four-barrel 429 V-8 packing 360 horsepower.

The Torino GT came with a 302-cubic-inch V-8, fake hood scoop, and steel wheels. Hidden headlamps, center console, and Laser side stripes were options. Engine upgrades included a 351 Cleveland four-barrel with 300 horses and the 370-horsepower Cobra Jet 429 with Ram Air induction.

These mid-size Fords could be blistering street performers. The 300-horsepower GT could go from 0-60 mph in about eight seconds. A 370-horse Cobra could do the same feat in about six seconds.

But the new styling proved less aerodynamically efficient in superspeedway racing compared to the 1968 and '69 Torinos. The concave backlight was said to be one of the problems. Ford had little choice but to run its older models in NASCAR, and it no longer had the services of Richard Petty, who had returned to the Plymouth camp. Ford took just six big-track wins, and by the end of the year would shutter most of its racing programs.

1970 MERCURY COUGAR ELIMINATOR

Cougar played the suave big brother to the rambunctious Mustang, but given the right motivation, the cat definitely had claws.

Mercury introduced its sporty coupe for 1967 as a luxury-touring alternative to the ponycar herd. It had mature styling and upscale interior appointments, and was built on a Mustang chassis stretched by three inches to provide a longer, ride-enhancing wheelbase.

Mercury in these years was deeply involved in racing. It backed a variety of record-setting Comet and Cougar drag specials, as well as NASCAR-winning Cyclones. Its street image was tamer, though not for lack of trying. Cougar contributed with the '68 GT-E, which like the Mustang opened the year with an available 390-horsepower 427 V-8, then switched to the 428 Cobra Jet.

Cougar's performance profile was raised by the April '69 introduction of the new Eliminator package. Taking cues from such rivals as the Z28 and SS Camaros, as well as the Boss 302 and Mach 1 Mustangs, Eliminator offered a range of engines, from the solid-lifter 302 to the 428 Cobra Jet. Like in the Mustang, the 428 was available in Drag Pak guise with an oil cooler and Detroit Locker rear end.

Cougar was mildly restyled for 1970, and the Eliminator returned for its final season. A 300-horsepower 351 was standard, with the Boss 302 or 335-horse 428 Cobra Jet optional. The standard hood scoop was only functional when ram air was ordered. A blackout grille, side stripes, and front and rear spoilers enhanced the purposeful look.

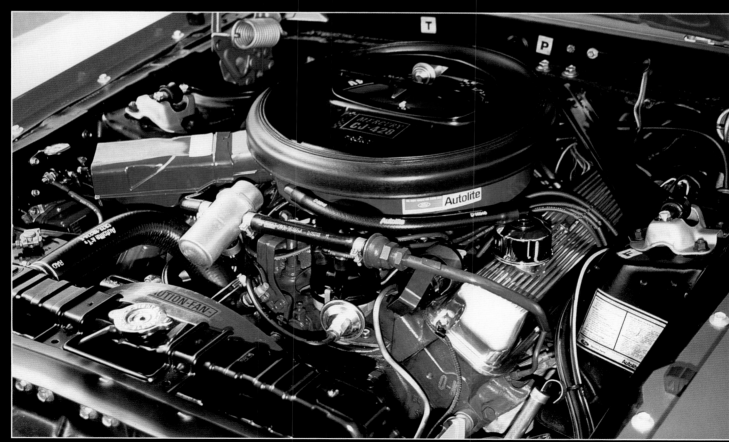

1970 OLDSMOBILE RALLYE 350

For 1970, Oldsmobile F-85 and Cutlass styling updates started with twin fine-mesh grilles. The portion of the hood that dropped between the grille sections now reached further down to meet a modified bumper. Bodysides were dramatically recontoured. The wheel-arch flares were removed, but most models now had a pronounced brow high up on the quarter panel above the rear wheel.

There was a new instrument panel too. It retained the three-dial layout, but now the gauges were placed in a flat panel that was recessed under the dash top. Under the hood, every Oldsmobile V-8 gained positive valve rotators to reduce carbon buildup and improve valve life.

A new budget-muscle Oldsmobile appeared—the W-45 "Rallye 350" package for F-85 two-door coupes, and Cutlass coupes and two-door Holiday hardtops. It included bold Sebring Yellow paint, black-and-red accents, yellow urethane-covered bumpers, blacked-out grilles, color-keyed Super Stock wheels with blackwall tires, FE2 performance suspension with front and rear stabilizer bars, sports-styled outside mirrors, dual exhausts, and a custom four-spoke sport steering wheel with a leather-like cover on the rim. A wild rear decklid spoiler was optional. The package also delivered the 4-4-2's available fiberglass hood with a pair of functional scoops and bright chrome tie downs. The engine was a 310-horsepower four-barrel 350 V-8 with air induction.

Some 3547 customers drove a Rallye 350 home, but the car shown here is one of only 30 that were made from the base F-85 coupe.

1970 PLYMOUTH AAR 'CUDA

Of course, the street AAR 'Cuda couldn't be mechanically identical to its Trans Am racing namesake. Unlike the Camaro Z28 and Mustang Boss 302, which were also built to homologate track cars, it didn't try to mimic the pavement-hugging posture of its competition cousin. Instead, Plymouth built a street rod.

The AAR 'Cuda took its title from Dan Gurney's All-American Racers, the team that ran Barracudas in the Sports Car Club of America's popular race series. Like the similar Dodge Challenger T/As, track AARs ran full-race 305-cubic-inch four-barrel V-8s and were lowered and modified for all-out twisty-course combat.

And like the production Challenger T/As built to qualify the cars for racing, street AARs used a 290-horsepower 340-cubic-inch small block with three two-barrel Holley carbs on an aluminum Edelbrock intake. Buyers could choose a four-speed or TorqueFlite, with a Sure-Grip axle and standard 3.55:1 gears. The engine breathed fresh air through a functional hood scoop.

The AAR's interior was basic 'Cuda, but its exterior certainly was not. From a matte-black fiberglass hood, through bodyside strobe stripes and tri-colored AAR shield, to the standard black rear spoiler, this was an exotic fish. Special shocks and rear springs raised the tail nearly two inches over regular 'Cuda specs, allowing clearance for exhaust pipes that exited in front of each rear tire.

The result of all this was an AAR 'Cuda better suited to a Saturday cruise night than a Sunday afternoon at Lime Rock. But the AAR was strong in a straight line, and an eyeful anywhere. Just like a good street rod.

1970 PLYMOUTH ROAD RUNNER SUPERBIRD

Spurred by Ford's fastback Torino Talladega and Mercury's Cyclone Spoiler II, Dodge added a wild aerodynamic nose cone and towering rear wing to the Charger 500 body to create the 1969 Dodge Charger Daytona. The Daytona was highly effective against its Ford and Mercury rivals in stock-car competition. Dodge's sister division Plymouth clamored for its own winged warrior, and got its wish in the 1970 Plymouth Road Runner Superbird.

Though it was a virtual twin to the Charger Daytona in concept, the Superbird's aerodynamic add-ons were developed expressly for the 1970 Plymouth Belvedere/Road Runner body. It was an exercise in savvy corporate parts swapping and cost-cutting ingenuity. The Superbird's front nose cone was fitted to the front fenders and a lengthened hood lifted from the 1970 Dodge Coronet.

As if a car with a huge rear wing and wind-tunnel-shaped snout weren't enough, Plymouth added cartoon Road Runner graphics, flat-black panels on the nose cone, and billboard-size "Plymouth" stickers on the rear flanks for even more visual punch. The visceral punch came courtesy of three engine choices: a four-barrel 440 with 375 horsepower, the "440+6" with 390, or the 426 Hemi.

The Superbird was a winner on the track, but not in the showroom. The outlandish bodywork was too much for many buyers, and a plain Road Runner was more than $1000 cheaper. Despite a production run of less than 2000 units, many Superbirds languished on dealer lots. Some dealers even stripped the aero add-ons and sold them as regular Road Runners.

1971 AMC HORNET SC/360

Even in 1970, muscle's pinnacle year, the signs were there for those who chose to look. Federal safety watchdogs, emissions regulators, insurance companies—even a changing social climate—all took aim at the high-performance car. For '71, the shots began to hit the target. Compression ratios retreated to accommodate low-lead fuel, gross horsepower ratings soon fell to tamer-sounding net figures, and public-relations-conscious automakers backpedaled.

Into this upheaval stepped AMC with a car that didn't deny the new reality. The Hornet was AMC's newest compact and the two-door sedan was a good start for a low-profile muscle car. Original plans called for both an SC/360 and an SC/401, but when AMC discovered that a 401-cubic-inch Hornet probably wouldn't provide much of an insurance edge, the 360 V-8 alone was borrowed from the company's Javelin AMX ponycar.

In standard form, the SC/360 had a two-barrel carb and a modest 245 horsepower. The $199 "Go" package added a four-barrel and a ram-air setup for a more satisfying 285 ponies. These were gross ratings. Optional in place of the standard three-speed manual was a Hurst-controlled four-speed or an automatic.

An SC/360 couldn't hang with the big-cube holdovers, but it did combine respectable quickness with a taut suspension, big tires, and a modestly sized package. The SC/360 turned out to be a sleeper in more ways than one. Even with a base price of just $2663, the car found only 784 buyers. The SC/360 died after just one year as one of the muscle era's better-kept secrets.

1971 BUICK GS 455

As the Seventies opened, at the forefront of the rush to horsepower was none other than Buick. Its performance offering was again based on the midsize Skylark, which received fresh styling for 1970. Replacing the GS 400 and its 400-cubic-inch V-8 was the GS 455, named for its new 455-cube engine.

The new mill offered not only the advantages of displacement, but also had bigger valves, better heads, and a hotter camshaft. In 1970, it was rated at 350 horsepower. Its prodigious 510 lb-ft of torque (at a mere 2800 rpm) was exceeded among production cars only by Cadillac's 472- and 500-cube V-8s.

Standard on GS models were functional hood scoops that mated to dual air-cleaner intakes. For the really power hungry, Buick offered the 455 Stage 1 performance package. Tweaks included a hotter cam, even larger valves with stronger springs, ported heads, and revised carburetor jetting. Torque was unchanged, and Buick slyly put horsepower at 360. Most testers said it was surely over 400. A steal at $199, the Stage 1 package included a Positraction 3.64:1 axle and mods to the available manual and automatic transmissions.

In 1971, all GS engines were detuned to run on low-lead fuel. There was just one GS series now; a 260-horsepower small-block Buick 350 was standard, and a 315-horse 455 was optional. Even the top-line Stage 1 455 was down to 345 ponies. Still, quarter-mile runs in the 14s were possible. Then the Stage 1's horsepower rating fell to 270 for '72. Any way you cut it though, Buick earned its place on muscle's all-time all-star team with the GS 455.

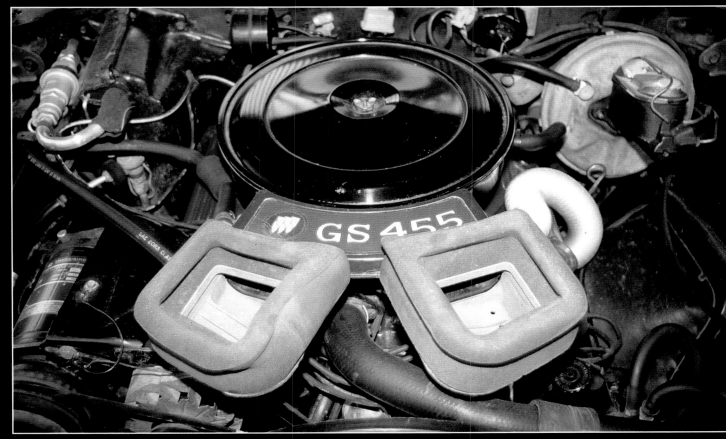

1971 CHEVROLET CAMARO Z28

The '67 was the first one and a sentimental favorite. A dual-carb, disc-brake Rally Sport '69 is arguably the most desirable. But the 1970 edition was simply the best all-around Z28 of all.

Camaro kept its 108-inch wheelbase for 1970, but otherwise underwent wholesale change with a new coupe body that was an instant classic. The Z28 returned as a $573 package, the heart of which was a new engine. Trans Am racing now allowed destroking to achieve 305 cubic inches, so the Z28 appropriated the Corvette's 350-cube LT1 V-8 as its sole powerplant. A timeless small block, the LT1 had solid lifters, a hot cam, big valves, 11.0:1 compression, and a 780-cfm Holley four-barrel. In the Z28 it was rated at 360 horsepower.

A $206 Hurst-shifted Muncie four-speed and $44 Positraction 3.73:1 gears were mandatory extras, and there was now enough low-end torque to offer the Z28's first automatic-transmission option. All '70 Camaros were good handlers, but the Z28 with its firmer underpinnings and sticky Polyglas F60×15 rubber was one world-class road car.

Hood and decklid striping, black grille, and mag-style steel wheels were part of the deal. A rear spoiler was standard, but the cowl induction hood was dropped. As before, Z28 could be combined with the Rally Sport package, which included a soft Endura grille surround and chrome bumperettes.

Changes for 1971 were modest. There were new front seats and a few tweaks, but the big news was that the LT1 was retuned and down to 330 ponies.

1971 PLYMOUTH GTX

The GTX was among the precious few 1971 muscle cars that needed no excuses. It was bold, it was bad. Some said it was beautiful.

Once again, the GTX played upscale companion to the budget-muscle Road Runner. Both were part of Chrysler's revamped midsize line (which also included the Dodge Charger), and both got curvaceous new "fuselage" styling on a wheelbase one inch shorter than before. With the new body came a three-inch increase in rear track, which benefitted handling, plus a reconfigured interior with a more comfortable driving position and superior ergonomics.

Although Mopar was the slowest of Detroit's Big Three to scale back, not all its V-8s escaped detuning. Road Runner's standard 383 four-barrel, for instance, lost 35 horsepower. GTX engines, however, held out relatively unscathed. Compression ratios were shaved a bit, but the standard 440 four-barrel and optional 440+6 lost only five horsepower, to 370 and 385. The seldom-ordered 426 Hemi held strong at 425 horses. Four-speeds and TorqueFlites, with axle ratios up to 4.10:1, were still available, as was the Air Grabber hood.

Weight was up by about 170 pounds, and quarter-mile times crept up higher, by nearly a full second in some tests. The '71 GTX also had the stiffest suspension of any Mopar intermediate, and most testers concluded that its handling wasn't good enough to justify the rock-hard ride.

Still, the GTX succumbed to the forces killing off hot cars, and '71 was its last year as a stand-alone model. At least it died with its big-cube boots on.

1971 PONTIAC GTO JUDGE

The styling of all midsize Pontiacs was significantly updated for 1970. GTOs received an all-new Endura nose with twin grille openings; disappearing headlamps were no longer offered. Sculpted bodysides featured attractive new character lines that flared out above the wheels, and the rear bumper was redesigned to house wraparound taillights. The big news was under the hood, where a 455-cubic-inch mill joined the carried-over 400s.

For 1971, there was another new nose, as well as a fresh hood. The most potent Ram Air engines were discontinued this year as GM lowered compression ratios. Judges packed the top GTO engine, the 335-horsepower 455 HO (for High Output). The '71 455 HO made less horsepower than the top '70 engine, the Ram Air IV 400, but made more torque at lower rpm. It was not exactly tractable, but was still better behaved on the street than the high-strung Ram Air IV.

Insurance rates and changing tastes caused total GTO production to dwindle to 10,532, and the Judge was retired in mid-1971 after just 374 had been built. That total included a mere 17 Judge convertibles.

For '72, the proud Goat was back to being an option package for the LeMans. It would die ignominiously as a trim package on the 1974 Ventura compact. The GTO made a surprising return to Pontiac's stable for 2004. Aside from rear-drive and a thumping V-8, the new GTO shared nothing with the legendary Great Ones of yore—it was an Americanized version of the Holden Monaro coupe that GM built in Australia. Sales were disappointing, and GTO retired again after 2006.

VIRGINIA 1972
BNP · 405

1972 FORD MAVERICK GRABBER

Ford entered 1970 with a new compact, the Maverick. It was much the same sort of car as Ford's original compact, the 1960 Falcon, and it had a similar mission: to counter small import models, sales of which had been creeping upward.

Predictably, Maverick was pitched as a roomier, more powerful, more trouble-free import alternative. Like Falcon, it had resolutely ordinary engineering. The 103-inch-wheelbase chassis had a typical leaf-spring live rear axle, twin-arm front suspension with coil springs, recirculating-ball steering, and drum brakes.

Under the hood it was 1961 all over again. The standard engine was the same 170-cubic-inch cast-iron six with 105 horsepower that had been optional in that year's Falcon. The familiar 200-cube enlargement of this workhorse was optional. The standard gearbox was a "three-on-the-tree" manual, and a three-speed Cruise-O-Matic was optional.

For '71 Maverick added a sporty two-door that was modishly called the Grabber. It had a jazzy two-tone hood with curious fake scoops, extra lamps in the grille with no round center emblem, plus dual racing mirrors and bodyside tape stripes. Floor shift and high-back bucket seats were new options.

The big news for 1972 was the first-time availability of the small-block 302 V-8 in the Maverick. It was only rated at 143 horsepower, but it was an especially good choice for the bestriped Grabber. A four-speed and disc brakes weren't available at any price though. At just $2309 to start, the Grabber wasn't a bad deal, costing some $400 less than a base Mustang.

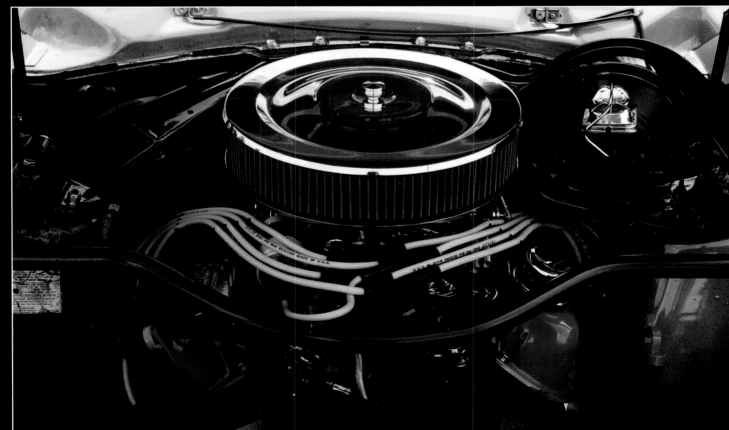

1972 OLDSMOBILE 4-4-2

Oldsmobile demoted the 4-4-2 to an appearance and handling option for select Cutlass models for 1972. Olds ads stressed the more affordable 4-4-2. It was available on base Cutlass coupe, Cutlass S coupe and hardtop, and Cutlass Supreme convertible. Package price was $71-$150 depending on the model—not a bad deal. The group included the expected stripe decals and badging, plus the FE2 suspension with heavy-duty front and rear stabilizer bars, Hurst shifter, 14×7-inch wheels, louvered hood, and special 4-4-2 grille.

All manufacturers now reported net horsepower and torque figures instead of gross ratings. The 4-4-2's standard engine was now a 160-horsepower 350-cubic-inch two-barrel V-8, with a 180-horse four-barrel version optional. The next step up was a four-barrel 455, which made 250 horsepower with the Turbo 400 automatic transmission and 270 with the M20 four-speed.

The top power option was still the W-30: a factory-blueprinted four-barrel 455 with 300 horsepower. Priced at a healthy $599, it again included a twin-scooped fiberglass Cold-Air induction hood.

The last 4-4-2 convertibles were built this year, as the body style would not be back for 1973. Total 4-4-2 production actually rose a bit over 1971, ending at 9845 units. Of those, only 772 were the W-30s.

In the all-new generation of Cutlasses that arrived for 1973, the formal-roof Supreme would drive its incredible success while the 4-4-2 continued to wane. Indeed, as muscle faded, Oldsmobile's best days were still ahead of it.

285

1973 CHEVROLET CHEVELLE SS

After five years on the same basic body shells, all General Motors interme-diates were totally new for 1973. Wheelbases held steady at 112 inches for two-door cars, and 116 inches for four-doors and wagons. Convertibles were dropped, and closed cars were dressed in new "Colonnade" styling. The two-door hardtops of the past were replaced by true coupes with thick B-pillars and fixed rear side-window glass.

The midsize Chevrolet Chevelle came in Deluxe, Malibu, and new upscale Laguna trim. Checking off option code Z15 and plunking down $243 would make an SS out of any Malibu coupe or—for the only time ever—station wagon equipped with a 350- or 454-cubic-inch V-8. Package equipment included a blacked-out grille, dual sport mirrors, color-keyed lower body striping, front and rear stabilizer bars, rally wheels, and G70×14 white-letter tires. SS identification showed up on the grille, front fenders, rear fascia (or wagon liftgate), steering wheel, and interior door panels.

The '73 350 engine was rated at 145 net horsepower with a two-barrel carb or 175 horses with a four-pot. The big-block 454 netted 245 ponies. Automatics were standard with the SS engines, but a four-speed could be ordered with the 454 and the chestier of the two 350s.

As it was, SS came to mean "Swan Song" in '73, even though 28,647 were ordered, an increase of almost 4000 from the 1972 total. The Laguna S-3 coupe then served as the sportiest Chevelle from 1974 to '76.

1973 DODGE CHARGER RALLYE

The 1971 Charger was a radical departure from its predecessor, losing two inches of wheelbase and gaining swoopy Coke-bottle contours. It now shared its body with the Super Bee, and though its performance leader retained the R/T designation, the only '71 Charger to come standard with the car's trademark hidden headlamps was the luxury SE version; they were otherwise optional.

But the R/T stayed true to its roots with a daunting underhood lineup. The 370-horsepower 440 four-barrel Magnum V-8 was standard, with the 385-horse 440 Six Pack available at extra cost. The 426 Hemi still topped the roster. A four-speed was standard, TorqueFlite was optional, and Hemi Chargers fed their dual quads with an Air Grabber-type scoop activated by a dashboard switch.

Mopar held out better against the anti-performance onslaught than most, but by 1972 it was in retreat too. The R/T, Super Bee, Six Pack, and Hemi all died, leaving the top Charger mill a 280-horsepower 440 four-barrel. A new Rallye option with a blackened hood bulge was now the default performance choice.

Still, as a product the Dodge Charger remained a success. Production didn't drop out of sight like that of so many rivals; model year 1973 set the all-time Charger production record of nearly 120,000 units. The '73s featured a new grille (no more hidden headlight option), fussier taillights, and larger rear quarter windows. The Rallye option package was back, but now included loud bodyside tape striping, hood tie-downs, and more complete Rallye instrumentation. The 340 small block made its final appearance.

1973 FORD GRAN TORINO SPORT

Among intermediate-class cars, Ford's Torino had been running second in sales to Chevrolet's Chevelle prior to 1972. The redesigned '72 Torino was larger than the car it replaced. A traditional perimeter frame isolated from the separate body by rubber body mounts replaced unibody construction. This, plus a redesigned suspension, resulted in a smoother ride. All Torinos had standard front disc brakes—a rarity in the early Seventies.

Torino buyers could choose a hardtop coupe, four-door sedan, or station wagon in base or Gran Torino trims. Gran Torinos had nicer interiors and a more distinctive grille. The Gran Torino Sport was the performance line, offered as a notchback hardtop or as a "SportsRoof" fastback that was reserved for only the Sport series. In addition, all Gran Torino Sports were V-8 powered. The bigger, better-riding Torino with attractive new styling was a hit and production increased by 52 percent over 1971. That was more than enough to put the Torino well ahead of archrival Chevelle.

The biggest change for 1973 was a new front end that was designed to satisfy the new federal requirement that cars withstand a five-mph crash without damage. Torino's sculpted 1972 front sheetmetal was replaced with a flat front end and a girderlike bumper. Engine choices for the Gran Torino Sport ranged from a 137-horsepower 302 up to a 219-horsepower 460 V-8 that was added midyear. The Sport still came in the same two body styles, but the SportsRoof, of which 51,853 of the '73s were made, put in its final appearance.

1973 PLYMOUTH DUSTER 340

Just as it had with the Road Runner in '68, Plymouth scored a budget-muscle bull's-eye in 1970 with the Duster 340. The formula was familiar. Take a cheap-to-build platform, in this case a Valiant wearing a new fastback body, and give it a hot engine, here Mopar's respected 340-cubic-inch V-8.

The determined little Duster was lighter, roomier, and faster than a 340 'Cuda. With a base price of just $2547, it was the lowest-priced car in Plymouth's Rapid Transit System. And the only one with front discs standard.

The 340 V-8 had proven itself over preceding years, powering a series of giant-killer Darts and earlier-generation Barracudas to mid-14-second ETs at near 100 mph. It was rated at 275 horsepower, but practiced observers insisted it actually made closer to 325 ponies. In the Duster, a heavy-duty three-speed manual was standard, with four-speed or TorqueFlite optional.

Other performance enhancers included a beefed suspension, front stabilizer bar, and E70×14 tires. Inside, buckets and a console with floor shift could be ordered in place of the standard bench. Outside, the hot-car cues were dual exhausts and modest decals.

For 1971, the 340 maintained its 275-gross-horsepower rating, but in net terms it was down to 240 for '72. The 1973s wore freshened front and rear styling, and Duster 340s sported revised striping. Engineering tweaks included a reworked front suspension and electronic ignition. The 340 four-barrel was still good for 240 ponies, and Duster 340's performance character remained intact.

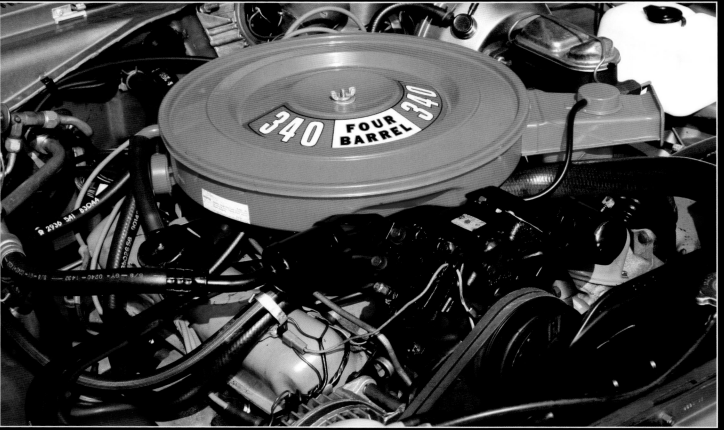

1974 CHEVROLET CAMARO Z28

A notable restyling gave the 1974 Camaro a "shovel" nose as well as new large, wraparound taillights to replace the previous round units. Both ends of the car now held five-mph impact bumpers that were made of spring-mounted aluminum, with resilient impact strips. The old split-bumper RS setup was retired. New "sugar scoop" headlights helped set the style direction for the rest of this Camaro generation that ended up running all the way through 1981.

The 1974 Z28 continued with the 1973 model's version of the 350. This meant it ran hydraulic rather than solid lifters, and the aluminum high-rise intake manifold was gone. Horsepower was 245 net.

Other performance hardware included a specially tuned suspension, Positraction rear end, and F60 boots. Buyers could choose a Muncie M21 four-speed or Turbo Hydra-matic. Bold hood and decklid stripes were a new $77 option.

After sales of 13,802 of the '74 models, the Z28 went on a brief hiatus. Enthusiasts applauded when the Z28 returned midway through the 1977 model year. It was now cataloged as a stand-alone model rather than an option package. The $5170 price tag included a raft of performance and image goodies, including tweaked suspension components, front and rear spoilers, and dual exhaust. Color-keyed wheels and bumpers, body striping, and blacked-out grilles and headlamp/parking light bezels further added to the exclusive look. Handling was a sharp as ever, but the 185-horsepower 350 couldn't provide the spirited acceleration of past Z28s.

1976 OLDSMOBILE 4-4-2

General Motors had looked to 1972 as the year for the corporation-wide remake of its midsized car brands, but as it turned out the new intermediates wouldn't be ready until the 1973 selling season.

Styling was much-modified for 1976, beginning with the adoption of quad headlamps for all models. All two-doors did away with the pronounced lower-body sculpting, but added a Toronado-like fenderline accent just aft of the doors. Grilles, too, were redone. Cutlass S models got a raked-back nose with two groups of nine vertical slots and headlights set back in "sugar scoop" bezels.

The 4-4-2 package used the Cutlass S for its base, and did away with the louvered hood and racing stripes on the hood and decklid. Lower bodyside stripes were much larger, however, and included the 4-4-2 identification as a graphic element. The $134 option package also included a beefier FE2 suspension.

Unfortunately, performance was not included with the 4-4-2 package. The standard engine in the Cutlass S was Chevrolet's 250-cubic-inch six with 105 horsepower. Then there was the 260-cubic-inch V-8 rated at 110 horsepower. Interestingly, it could be mated to a new 5-speed manual transmission with an overdrive top gear. Then came the Oldsmobile 350 V-8 with a four-barrel carburetor and 170 horsepower. Top dog was the once-mighty 455 V-8, now rated at 190 horsepower. It would be replaced by a 403-cube Olds V-8 for 1977.

Cutlass production broke the half-million mark for the first time in 1976. Sales figures for the 4-4-2 are not available.

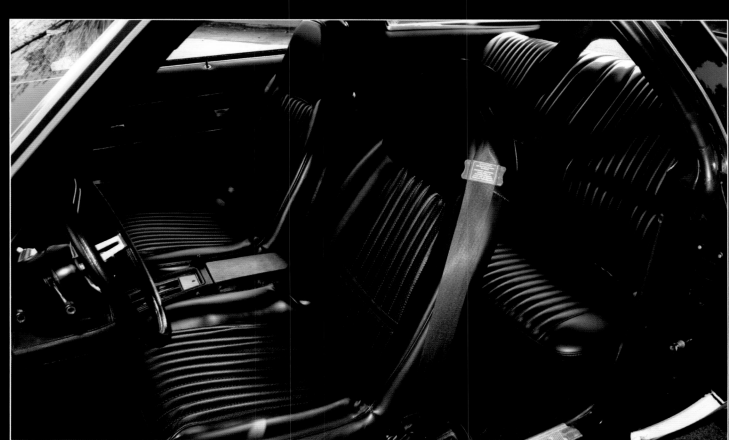

1978 FORD MUSTANG II KING COBRA

Ten years after its debut, Ford's Mustang received a comprehensive redesign. The resulting car—the Mustang II—was loved by many and hated by some. Oddly enough, each camp had valid points and both might have been right.

Lee Iacocca and his boss, Henry Ford II, decided that for 1974, Mustang would become smaller, less bulky, and more refined. The Mustang II was 18.8 inches shorter than the 1973 model, almost four inches narrower, and nearly 500 pounds lighter. The Mustang II used much of the subcompact Pinto's unibody structure as a base, but added a front subframe and better rear springs.

At introduction, the only performance-themed model was the Mach 1 hatchback with a 105-horsepower 2.8-liter V-6 and some appearance items including black accent paint. The 1975 models added a V-8 option, but it was a 122-horsepower 302 that could only be mated to a three-speed automatic.

As the Seventies progressed, the public's taste for performance resurfaced, but expectations had clearly changed. The 1976 Mustang II added a four-speed option for the otherwise unchanged 302 V-8. There was also a new $325 Cobra II appearance package for any base hatchback, even if it had four-cylinder power.

Mustang II made its last appearance for 1978. One highlight was an expressive King Cobra package with a standard 139-horsepower 302 V-8. The new option package listed for $1253 and was heavy on serpent imagery. A deep wraparound airdam, deck spoiler, hood scoop, and a big Cobra decal for the hood were part of the deal too. Quarter-window louvers and a T-bar roof were extra.

1979 PONTIAC FIREBIRD TRANS AM

Yet another new look greeted Firebird shoppers in 1979, thanks to a dramatic front and rear facelift. Each of the four headlights was mounted in its own inset bezel, and the large urethane nose had its split-grille treatment set low at bumper level. At the rear, there was a full-width taillamp with a blacked-out cover.

Regular Trans Ams used an Oldsmobile-built 403-cubic-inch V-8 that was rated at 185 horsepower. But there was a final batch of Pontiac 400-cube V-8s that were good for 220 horsepower and were stuffed under the hoods of the 10th Anniversary Trans Am specials. The 400 engine was marked by "T/A 6.6" decals on the shaker hood scoop. Wearing silver and charcoal paint, silver hatch-roof panels, matching silver-leather upholstery, and unique dished wheels, the limited-edition cars sold for a whopping $10,620. It was the first Firebird to sticker for more than 10 grand, yet 7500 were sold.

In addition, 109,609 regular Trans Ams found buyers, and this accounted for more than half of the year's total Firebird output. It was Firebird's best sales season, with 211,454 rolling off the assembly line.

The Eighties would bring a new turbocharged 301-cubic-inch V-8 engine rated at 210 horsepower, and optional four-wheel disc brakes. Serious muscle would eventually return in later third- and fourth-generation Firebird models, but sales never matched the impressive totals of the late Seventies. The Firebird was dropped after the 2002 model year, and Pontiac itself was shuttered after 2009. With that, the marque that essentially created the muscle car was history.

1987 BUICK GRAND NATIONAL

Truth be told, the first 1982 Buick Grand Nationals were more show than go. The package consisted of a charcoal-gray-and-silver paint job with red accent stripes, blacked-out body trim, front air dam, rear spoiler, T-top roof, and Grand Touring suspension on what was an ordinary midsize Regal coupe.

The idea here was to capitalize on Buick's success in NASCAR Grand National racing. Big decals spelled out Buick on the rear flanks, while "Grand National" and turbo V-6 badges were found on the front fenders. Very few of the cars carried a turbocharged V-6 engine though, and most had a naturally aspirated 4.1-liter Buick V-6 rated at 125 horsepower.

Grand National made its second appearance for 1984. Performance was a consideration this time, and the GN now came standard with a 200-horsepower turbocharged 3.8-liter V-6. The 1986 Grand Nationals added an intercooler and a new two-piece intake manifold to the turbo V-6 for a big horsepower boost.

The 1987 models were tweaked further still, and were now rated at 245 horsepower and 355 pound-feet of torque. Period road tests quoted a 0-60 mph time of about 6.0 seconds, and quarter-mile times in the mid 14s. This was fast by any standard of the day, and Grand National had five more horsepower than the contemporary Corvette's 5.7-liter V-8.

What started as a flashy commemoration of Buick's surprising success in stock-car racing quickly transformed into a full-on muscle car. And more significantly, the Grand National pointed the way to the future of high performance.